CHARLOTTE BROWNE

ULTIMATE FOOTBALL HEROES

SMITH

FROM THE PLAYGROUND TO THE PITCH

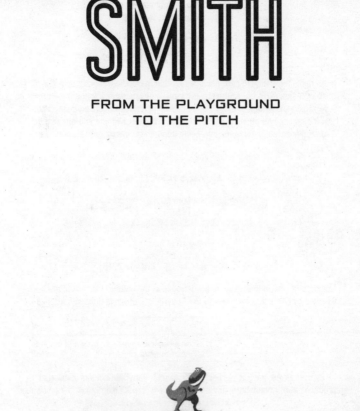

DINO

Published by Dino Books,
an imprint of John Blake Publishing,
2.25, The Plaza,
535 Kings Road,
Chelsea Harbour,
London SW10 0SZ

www.johnblakebooks.com

www.facebook.com/johnblakebooks
twitter.com/jblakebooks

This edition published in 2018

ISBN: 978 1 78606 971 9

British Library Cataloguing-in-Publication Data:

A catalogue record for this book is available from the British Library.

Design by www.envydesign.co.uk

Printed and bound in Great Britain by Clays Ltd, Elcograf S.p.A.

3 5 7 9 10 8 6 4 2

John Blake Publishing is an imprint of Bonnier Books UK
www.bonnierbooks.co.uk

To my older brother Richard, for being such a good sport – and for patiently explaining the key differences between football league tables to me – I think I finally get that the European Champions League has absolutely no connection to the Championship League.

ULTIMATE
FOOTBALL HEROES

Charlotte Browne knew from a young age she would probably
end up working with words. She has worked as a journalist for a
number of publications, from *The Independent* to *Prima*, and written
for organisations within the not-for-profit and charity sectors.
She is probably at her happiest walking Cornish countryside,
swimming in the sea or playing her favourite songs on piano.
She lives in south London.

Cover illustration by Dan Leydon.
To learn more about Dan visit danleydon.com
To purchase his artwork visit etsy.com/shop/footynews
Or just follow him on Twitter @danleydon

TABLE OF CONTENTS

CHAPTER 1

WATFORD BABY

It was a cold winter's day in the village of Garston in Watford. As Bernard Smith held his two-month-old baby Kelly in his lap, he settled down to listen to the Saturday football results. Christmas 1978 wasn't far away, but Bernard and his wife Carol hadn't had much time to think about it as they adjusted to life with their firstborn Kelly – there was still a lot to get used to.

Thankfully Bernard's sister Beryl lived just around the corner and had invited them over for Christmas – so cooking a turkey was one less thing to worry about this year. Carol looked over and smiled at Bernard who had a worried expression on his face.

He wasn't thinking about Christmas, he had the footie results on his mind. He shook his head in frustration as he heard Watford FC's results for the afternoon. He'd been hoping for a win.

'Shall I take her, Bernard? I think she's due a feed,' said Carol.

'No, hold on a while, eh... I think she's alright,' replied Bernard. He loved hugs with his baby daughter and bonding with her as much as possible, especially while listening to dismal football results – she helped to ease these tense moments.

'I thought Taylor was going to do great things with our club, Carol, but we're still in the fourth division!'

'Give him a chance, Bernard, he's only been in the job five minutes!'

'Well, nearly a year, actually Carol, but you're right... Watford will rise again,' he said smiling. 'I've every faith. We'll be in the FA Cup within six years. Then who knows – the Premier League within ten?'

'Er, yes dear,' said Carol, hopefully. She didn't quite share his optimism, or enthusiasm, as she turned back to ironing Kelly's babygrow.

Bernard switched his attention back to Kelly. Blissfully unaware of any football results, she looked into her dad's eyes and wriggled her fists and legs playfully in the air. He rocked her in his arms and chanted 'Watford till I die'. He held her out in front of him and gave her more room to kick.

'She's got strong legs on her this one, Carol,' he said, 'she's already trying to stand up by herself – she's not even two months!'

'You're telling me, you didn't carry her!' replied Carol, 'She was always kicking in there!'

Bernard turned to look at his wife and beamed. 'Maybe she'll play for Watford FC one day...' He looked back to Kelly whose eyes widened as he nodded his head at her.

'Don't be daft, Bernard,' replied Carol, 'she's a girl.'

Under her breath she muttered: 'I hope not, they're rubbish.'

'Now don't you be sexist!' teased Bernard. 'We're in the age of women's lib, aren't we? Girls are doing all sorts of things they've been told they couldn't do before... running marathons, running businesses...

You know what, we could even have one running the country by next May!' He added: So why shouldn't girls play football?!'

'Yes, alright Bernard... but it's not very likely, is it?' She shook her head somewhat regretfully. Her husband was a huge fan of football and she knew he'd love to pass that down to his children. She hoped he'd have a son he could share that love and passion for the sport with one day.

She thought for a minute and said: 'I certainly don't know any women who play football, that's for sure. No girls at my school ever played it either. I was mean on the netball pitch though, I can tell you... they didn't stand a chance with me in wing attack!'

Bernard turned to a frustrated Kelly who was still trying to force her strong legs up to stand on his lap. 'Now don't you listen to your mother, sweetheart – you wanna be a footballer, you be one, be whatever you want to be.' Kelly looked back at him and gave what he thought was a smile.

'She's smiling Carol! See, she agrees!'

'Oh, it's just wind, Bernard...'

CHAPTER 2

BORN TO PLAY

'Hello Bernard, hello Carol!' Aunt Beryl arrived
at the holiday chalet the family had all rented for
a summer getaway in Clacton-on-Sea, clutching a
present. It was a chance for the whole family to get
away and unwind and take in the fresh sea air. Kelly
had recently learnt to walk, and Bernard was looking
forward to taking her down to the beach. Carol had
also recently given birth to their second child, Glen
and needed a decent break away. Aunt Beryl cooed
at the newborn who was being rocked gently in his
mother's arms. 'Isn't he gorgeous?! You must both be
so proud. You look tired though Carol... can I take
him for you?'

'Well yes, Kelly is moving around a lot now. It's hard work having a toddler and a baby, I can barely keep up with her. Obviously with Bernard at work, it can be tough.'

'Where is she anyway, Carol? I've got a present for her.'

'Oh thank you Beryl, you are generous.' Carol secretly hoped it wasn't another doll though, Kelly just wasn't very interested in them and a pile of them had started to build up at the Smiths' household.

Beryl looked out of the window where Kelly was toddling round the garden with her dad. The little girl still wasn't perfect on her feet and fell over a few times, but she moved with speed and quickly got back up each time. Beryl noticed with surprise, though, that Kelly was in control of a plastic ball, pursuing it with dogged determination, concentration and even skill. The ball seemed to be permanently attached to the toddler's feet these days.

'Good grief, Carol – have you seen this?' exclaimed Beryl. 'She's even better with that ball than when I saw her last.'

'You know what, pretty much from the time she took her first steps, she seemed to be looking around for something to kick. I had a ball of wool that I couldn't find anywhere... next thing I know Bernard's calling out to me – she was practically dribbling it across the floor!

Beryl went out to the garden. Bernard was at one end of the garden calling to Kelly, encouraging her to kick the plastic ball. 'Come on Kell, keep going, keep going!' Kelly's gaze was fixated on the ball as she dribbled it across the grass towards her father. Her face broke out into a smile as she made it to him without falling over. He then switched to the other side of the lawn and encouraged her to come back the other way.

'Don't tire her out too much, Bernard!' called Carol.

'She loves it, Carol!' This time he moved towards her as though to tackle her. Instinctively, Kelly tried to move the ball away from his challenge. Giggling, she nudged the ball between his legs and then toddled to the left of him. Beryl and Carol gasped in disbelief.

'Way to go, Kelly!' said Bernard. 'Would you look at that, getting around her own dad!' He picked her up to give her a celebratory hug. She didn't want to be held for long, though, and wriggled to get down and back to the ball as soon as possible.

'Amazing! Now look what I've got for you!' Beryl handed her a dolly.

'Isn't she pretty? What would you like to call her?'

Kelly looked at her aunt quizzically. She looked back at her dad, then tottered hurriedly over to the ball, which had rolled into a bush.

Bernard looked at his sister's puzzled face and shrugged. 'Sorry Beryl, I just don't think she's that interested.'

There was a knock at the door as Bernard's lifelong friend Russ Cawson appeared.

'Hello Kelly! My word, haven't you grown?!' He ran out towards her to say hello. 'But more importantly, how much stronger are those legs of yours getting?' Kelly ran behind her dad's legs, initially a little shy.

'She's a bit wary sometimes,' said Bernard. 'Give

her five minutes or so.' Kelly knew she recognised Russ from somewhere, He was someone who would always spend time kicking a ball to her.

'I think I know what might bring her out of her shell.' Russ smiled and brought something out from behind his back – a real football.

'Oy!' protested Bernard. 'You've beaten me to it, I brought one with us to take down the beach!'

Kelly's face peeped out from behind her dad's legs and lit up as she saw the ball. Her curiosity was stirred. It was small, with the Nike logo across it, but she immediately knew that it was bigger than the little plastic ball she'd been shuffling around all afternoon.

Smiling, Russ stretched the ball out to her. She moved towards him expectantly, then looked up, as if to say, 'Well, come on then!'

'I've heard you're getting very good with the ball, Kelly!'

'Go on Kelly, show him your skills,' said Bernard.

Russ went to roll the ball towards her – then he gently kicked it at the last minute. With a big smile,

Kelly toddled towards it and right on time kicked the ball in mid-air back to him.

'That was a touch and a half!' exclaimed Russ. 'Great contact!'

'She's brilliant!' exclaimed Beryl.

'That's my girl', said Bernard beaming. 'She really has got something special, hasn't she?'

Carol watched from the back door with baby Glen in her arms. She called out happily: 'You know what, Bernard, you might yet have your Watford player!' She looked back at Glen. 'It'll take the pressure off you eh?'

CHAPTER 3

ONE OF THE LADS

Kelly sat in class and stared dejectedly at the blackboard ahead of her, trying to make sense of the sums on the blackboard. She'd hated maths in infant school but now she was at Lea Farm Junior, just five minutes away from her home in Fourth Avenue. It was still her least favourite subject. Her best mate Graham sat next to her and looked just as bored. They were both itching to get off their seats.

Her teacher could tell her attention had drifted. 'Kelly, can you tell me what...?' The bell for morning break interrupted her. Within a second, Kelly was up and out of her chair, followed enthusiastically by Graham and a string of boys.

'Kelly!!!' But Miss Perkins knew it was no use. She was gone in a flash, headed towards the playground already in control of the ball, dribbling around the lads trying to challenge her. She looked at the other girls heading out to play skip rope and hopscotch. Kelly had given up asking any of them to play football with her a long time ago. In class, she was quite shy and didn't speak a lot, but she came out of her shell when she had a ball at her feet. She was in charge and always seemed to have control of the game.

One of the lads shouted: 'Kelly – come on!!! Let us have the ball!'

'You'll have to get it off me!' retorted Kelly. She dribbled around two lads who tried to challenge her.

'King of the square! King of the square!' shouted several of the lads in unison.

'Oh okay then.' Kelly relented, with a smile.

'King of the square' was one of her favourite games. There was a big wall at the end of the playground, which was great practice for all of them.

'One touch – just one touch on the ball!' This was the only rule. Kelly enjoyed sticking to it and loved setting continuous goals for herself. Graham went up first and kicked the ball over the wall. 'Out, out!' they all shouted. He went and sat down looking fed up. Kelly was up next.

'Hang on... let's make this harder.' Kelly grabbed a chalk and drew a triangle on the wall. 'Hit the ball in there!' The boys groaned. Graham threw the ball to her and she kicked it into the triangle, with one touch.

'Can't we just hit the wall?'

'Oh come on', replied Kelly, 'don't you want to get better?!'

Kelly secretly kept a tally for every time she managed to get the ball in the triangle. She sensed the boys got a bit funny about it when she made it too competitive against them. She wondered if this was because she often beat them. She didn't gloat about it – it wasn't in her nature to boast – but she knew she was just as good as them, if not better. They carried on, trying different shapes on the wall too – circles and squares.

Miss Perkins noticed her doing this in the breaks.

She said to Bernard: 'I don't know much about football, but she really pushes herself when she plays, you know. She's definitely not lazy.'

'I know,' said Bernard with pride. 'She's actually very technical, always trying to improve her skills.'

*

'Kelly, Kelly – we want Kelly!'

Kelly ran over happily to join the Lea Farm School football team. She was always at least the first or second to get picked out by the captain, and never felt different because she was a girl. She was their equal on the pitch.

As far as the boys were concerned, Kelly really was just 'one of the lads'. She was disappointed there were never any girls in her class to play football with, but there were some plus points – she had to work that bit harder to compete with the boys who tended to be faster on the pitch than her. With all her wall practice, she was just as technically minded as them, though, if not more so.

'Where do you want me, Jake?!' she called.

From the age of just eleven, Kelly found herself

falling naturally into the role of midfielder. Here, she developed a an aptitude for keeping the opponents back but doing what she loved best – getting up front on the attack. She was a natural athlete who could run and gain speed quickly.

One day they played a friendly against Cherry Tree Primary School. The boys soon discovered it wasn't wise to doubt the skill of this girl, who had no fear as she ran towards them.

Kelly received the ball at first touch from her teammate. She started to dribble it down towards the defence. 'Wow!' she thought to herself as the pitch stretched out ahead of her. 'It looks absolutely massive... how am I gonna get it down there?!'

What would her dad say? She imagined him speaking to her. 'Concentrate on the ball Kell, you know you can get past these lads.'

Kelly kept dribbling and dodging the midfielders. Once she got past them she saw she still had half a field to get down. The goalkeeper looked like a little dot in the distance. But he was darting around clearly concerned by the girl heading towards him at speed. As Kelly steered past the defence, more space opened up for her. There wasn't much more time to think and she knew instinctively she should just go for it – she saw the goalie move to the right and, quick as anything, her left foot went for the strike into the right of the net, straight past him. GOAL!

'Yes!!!' Her teammates ran over and jumped around her in celebration. One opponent certainly wasn't joining in, though. He'd tried to challenge Kelly just before she shot on target. Unfortunately for him, he'd got in the way of Kelly's left boot and was now hobbling off to the side. 'He's bleeding!' squawked one of his teammates.

'Shouldn't have tried to tackle Kelly!' cried Graham, as they all patted her on the back.

One parents' evening, Bernard and Carol chatted to Miss Perkins about Kelly. The teacher said: 'She's a good all-rounder in her subjects, even maths when she bothers to apply herself. It's just not what she naturally enjoys.'

'No', agreed Bernard. 'But I know what she *does* enjoy.' His eyes twinkled.

Miss Perkins smiled. 'Yes, she excels at PE and is a natural athlete in all sports. But you know, she's never happier than when she has a ball at her feet.'

'She was born to do it.'

'You know what, I think you're right, Mr Smith. I honestly can't see her doing anything else in the future. It's just a shame there's no real career in it...'

In the car on the way back home, Kelly's parents reflected on their conversation with Miss Perkins.

Carol said: 'I really don't want her other subjects to suffer, Bernard.'

'Where there's a will, there's a way. And she has plenty of will. And so much passion for the game. Just see how she runs rings around those lads in the playground!'

'I know, I just don't want her to get her hopes dashed, Bernard, out there in the real world.'

CHAPTER 4

PRACTICE MAKES PERFECT

One Sunday morning Graham called for Kelly. He wanted to take her down to Garston Boys Football Club, where he played.

'Come and watch me play, Kelly!'

'Oh great, you get to play and I just watch? That doesn't sound much fun.'

At least when the team found themselves a player down, she got a chance to show off her skills on the pitch. Glad not to have wasted her Sunday, she flew around the pitch, blending in among the boys.

Dick Bousefield, who ran the team, was impressed by what he saw. He ran over to speak to her at half-time.

'Hello! You did great out there! What's your name?'

Kelly was flush-faced from running up and down the pitch and was suddenly a bit taken aback by the attention.

'Er, Kelly, sir.'

'Kelly?! That's... oh! Right!'

With her tomboy-esque short haircut, a lot of people assumed Kelly was a boy, especially when they saw her running around on the pitch. So she looked down at the ground, a little embarrassed. This was typical, it happened a lot. She just hoped it wouldn't affect her playing football.

Dick gave her a big smile. 'Okay, well, Kelly, how'd you like to join the team, then?'

'Really?' said Kelly. 'As in, get to wear the kit and everything?'

'Yes – of course!'

Back at home, Kelly flew in through the back door, startling her mum who was cooking their tea.

'Dad! Guess what??!' Bernard looked up from the TV. 'They want me for the team!'

'Who, what??'

'Garston Boys! They want me to play for them!'

'Well, of course they do!' He jumped up and hugged her. They were both delighted and jumped around the living room cheering.

*

From that point on, Kelly lived for Sundays. She jumped out of bed at the crack of dawn because she was so excited to play football in all seasons – whether it was freezing cold or boiling hot. With pride, she looked over at the kit. The shirts were striped blue and black, with black shorts. The football grounds were a short ride away in the car. On the way, she chatted excitedly to her dad.

'I can't believe it – my first proper kit!'

'Well, you're good enough to be wearing it, Kelly. And it looks smashing.'

Bernard was happy to be her taxi, because it was so great to see her so excited. She was up, long before he ever was on a Sunday, looking forward to the playing ahead.

'I know, dad, I know.' She was a bit nervous. She

knew she could play well but she'd be up against the best of the boys in her area.

As if reading her mind, Bernard looked over and said: 'You're as good as any of them, Kelly – a lot better, in fact.'

Out on the pitch, this proved to be true. It didn't take long for Dick to see her potential, as both a midfielder and a striker. Her practice had really paid off and paid dividends. There was rarely a time when she was without control of the ball – she could receive it at first touch, dribble past defenders and deliver goals for the team.

'Technically, she outstrips them all,' said Dick to Bernard. 'Is she just naturally brilliant?'

Bernard watched her proudly from the sidelines. 'Yes. But she works really, really hard at it too.'

He thought back to a conversation with his wife earlier that morning at home.

'Carol, where's my set of golf balls?'

'Well, I don't know, Bernard, they should be where you last had them.'

'Oh, of course...' Bernard peeped his head out

of the backdoor to see Kelly dribbling one around a line of cones in the yard with a look of intense concentration on her face.

'Kelly, what you doing? Isn't a football good enough, you can't go round nicking my golf balls too.'

'It's really good practice, dad! Honest!'

He looked at the wall. Beach balls, soft balls, footballs, Kelly was practising with all sorts of different weights, shapes and sizes to improve her skills.

'Got to improve my touch, dad!' she said. He couldn't disagree with that.

Other times, he'd look out of the window and see her juggling a hacky sack and dribbling in the garden. He could see that she was completely lost in the moment and was visualising herself on the football pitch.

Kelly's hard work and dedication had the chance to shine in an eleven-a-side match. It also gave her the chance to experience her first home and away games.

'We're playing away next Sunday, dad! With a side called Evergreen!'

Out on the pitch, Kelly dominated the field. Bernard watched from the sidelines with Barry, an old friend of his whose son was also playing. Barry turned to Bernard and said:

'Who's that kid? He's brilliant, isn't he? On both his left and right foot! My Kevin's not going to be too happy though... he hasn't been able to get the ball off him once!'

Bernard smiled and said: 'That's not a boy. That's Kelly, my daughter.'

'What? Flippin' 'eck!' Barry called out to his son. 'Kevin, Kevin!!! Pull your finger out – that's a girl who's running rings around you!'

Kelly looked over at her dad and pulled a face. Kevin hung his head and kept running.

On the way back in the car, Kelly was deep in thought. The she piped up. 'Why did he have to say that dad? It was so embarrassing.'

'I know, love, try not to let it get to you, just concentrate on doing what you love doing, playing football.'

'It's so unfair, if there were girls to play with, I'd

play with them. But there aren't.'

'I know, but you shouldn't have to, you're as good as any of them.'

'Doesn't make any difference though, does it?'

CHAPTER 5

KICKED OUT THE CLUB

Kelly was out in the garden one Sunday setting herself new targets with her keepy-uppies.

'I did fifty yesterday,' she said to herself. 'Fifty-five today!' As with the ball practise she was always setting new goals. And despite some funny looks from the parents at Garston Boys, she was looking forward to the second half of the season. She was so engrossed in her keepy-uppies she didn't notice her dad at the back door or when he spoke her name. She dropped the ball, then turned to look at him.

'Fifty-nine, dad! Fifty-nine! I beat my target.'

Her dad smiled wearily back at her.

'Dad, what is it?'

'I've got some bad news Kell. I've just spoken to Mr Bousefield.'

Kelly's face fell. She saw her mum behind him, looking upset.

'I'm afraid they're going to have to take you off the team. None of the other teams will play if you are.'

'But Dad! What?! Why?!'

'It's because the matches are just friendlies, there's nothing he can do. He's annoyed as anything about it Kell.'

Kelly kicked the ball against the fence with sheer frustration.

'If there were just some girls I could play with! It's so unfair!!!'

Bernard and Carol were used to hearing this phrase come out of their children's mouths, for all sorts of different reasons – from not being allowed to stay up late to being forced to eat their greens. But on this occasion they both completely agreed with Kelly.

'No Kelly, it's not fair,' said Bernard. He hugged his daughter as she burst into tears on his shoulders.

'I just want to play football, dad!'

'I know Kelly, and you will. We'll find a way.'

*

Kelly felt sad for weeks afterwards, but was cheered up by her friends at school who rallied around her.

'You can't go to waste, Smudge, you're one of the best midfielders out there!'

'We don't score half as much now at Garston, it's rubbish.'

'We miss you, Smithy.'

She really missed Sundays too, playing football. She still played during breaks and bossed Glen around in the garden or the lounge playing one-on-one, but it wasn't the same as playing with a kit on – somehow it felt more real that way and at Garston Boys, she had felt as though she had been taken seriously.

Kelly had made a new group of friends playing football at her senior school Francis Combe. They also thought her situation was unfair, and told her about Herons, a football club they all attended down by Harebreaks Recreation Ground in Watford. They arranged for her to have a trial there and she was ecstatic to be selected. Her parents were happy to see her so eager to get out playing again on a Sunday. Bernard didn't even mind being back on taxi duty!

This is great, thought Kelly, as she ran up and down the pitch on the attack. But she soon became aware of the unhappy expressions on the faces of parents on the sidelines, especially when she caught the ball off one of their sons. One Sunday, she noticed a big crowd had gathered, more people than usual. She suspected they'd come to see her – the ultra-skilled 'wonder kid' they'd heard about. This filled her with pride, but also a sense of dread.

She managed to retrieve the ball off an opponent when she was in the penalty box.

She heard someone shout: 'Foul! Bad tackle!'

Head down, she tried to ignore it and concentrate on the game. But she misjudged when to pass to her teammate a few times and missed a few opportunities to take shots on target.

The jibes continued. 'What's she doing here anyway?! Shouldn't she be playing with My Little Pony?!'

'Get her off the pitch!'

Kelly tried to concentrate. 'They're just jealous, keep going,' she told herself. But she couldn't believe it was grown-ups being mean, rather than the kids. She kept her head down the rest of the game and tried to cut the voices out, but lost control of the ball a few times and fell over due to a particularly hard tackle.

'Oh dear love, bit rough for you is it?!' she heard one guy shout. She looked over and saw her dad having stern words with him. She cringed inside – how embarrassing, now her dad was getting involved. Tears of anger and frustration filled her eyes. She hated unnecessary attention at any time, but she hated it even more on the pitch when she just wanted to score goals. She didn't want to show it had got to her, but she'd had enough.

She made it to the end of the game then ran off the pitch, straight past her dad. In the car on the way back she was silent for most of the journey. Finally she said: 'I don't want to do it anymore, Dad.'

'Well Kelly, their manager just spoke to me.

I asked him if he could have a word with those idiots and he said your presence is "upsetting the atmosphere", so they've got to let you go. I'm sorry, love. I can't believe this is happening again.'

Back home, Kelly ran upstairs and flung herself down on her bed. Even her favourite meal – Carol's shepherd's pie – couldn't tempt her down the stairs that night.

Bernard knocked on her door. 'Don't let them get to you, Kelly.'

'Go away!'

Carol shook her head. 'You know what, Bernard, she's good at so many other sports, not just football. Her netball teacher says she can make the County Trials easily.'

'I know Carol, but it's football she loves isn't it, she's obsessed. And she should be able to play.'

*

Netball was one sport where Kelly did get a chance to play with the girls. She blended in and felt a little bit less of an outsider.

'Great catch, Kelly!' Her teacher appreciated her

natural athleticism during any netball game. Kelly loved the speed of play but was a little fed up in goal defence position. She was an attacker at heart and got bored stopping the opposition from scoring goals. There just wasn't quite enough running around for her either.

Her teacher spotted her frustration. 'How about we talk about changing your position when you play for the county, eh Kelly?'

Kelly thought for a minute. Did she want to give up more weekend time that she could devote to practising football? She did like netball but knew what she'd rather be doing. And the uniform... she looked down at the green, flared bottle skirt flapping around her legs and looked back at her teacher.

'Nah, I don't think so, Miss. Thanks, but I'd rather be in a pair of shorts!'

CHAPTER 6

HIGHBURY HEROES

Saturday was an exciting day for Kelly. If she wasn't Playing football she was gearing up to watch the Premier League teams play on TV. Bernard was a Watford FC fan and although they'd risen up the ranks over the years she hadn't witnessed the team do much since their glory days of winning the 1984 FA Cup Final.

Her dad said: 'Loyalty Kell... it's about loyalty.'

'Yeah yeah, Dad, they're just not that good though are they?'

Her brother Glen was a Liverpool fan, but it was Arsenal that won Kelly's heart from an early age.

One Saturday afternoon there was a knock at the

front door. It was Russ Cawson, Bernard's best mate. Bernard grinned from ear to ear when he saw him. Kelly looked up for a second – she was waiting for her favourite TV show, *Football Focus*, to start.

'Is she ready, Bernard?' Russ said.

'I think she will be, Russ.'

'Well she can't go like that, she's gonna have to change into the Gunners' kit.'

'What?' Kelly watched in awe as Russ unravelled the red Arsenal home strip with JVC across the front. 'You'll be needing this for Highbury!'

'But it's Arsenal versus Liverpool today?!'

'Yeah, you're seeing it live.'

'No way!' Kelly leapt up and down.

She couldn't contain her excitement on the way there. She'd seen so many of these matches on the TV, but there was nothing that could prepare her for the atmosphere at the match. Over 40,000 fans cheering on their home team – her spine tingled with excitement as they waited for the players to come out. It was a great time for Arsenal who were on their way to winning the league again. Kelly couldn't believe she was seeing these incredible players running around on the pitch in action, for real, in front of her own eyes – they were only ever little dots on the TV at home.

'Russ! Look, there's Paul Merson!' She spotted the Number 10 walking out, a position she longed to play professionally one day. What an incredible buzz. She was there, just before he headed their first goal into the net against Liverpool, after a corner kick. After Lee Dixon scored a penalty she saw Alan Smith put in the final strike after a great back heel from Merson. They put the match to bed.

From then on, Kelly knew she'd always be an Arsenal fan. She especially looked up to Ian Wright who joined Arsenal later on:

'He's got such energy, Dad!'

She stared at the TV, transfixed. Wright looked as though he was having so much fun out on the pitch, more than any of them.

'You can't call yourself a real Arsenal supporter, though, Kell,' Bernard teased. 'You idolise that young Ryan...'

It was true. She did. How she wished Giggs played for Arsenal, rather than Manchester United. She videotaped all his matches so she could study his moves. She particularly loved to watch the match where Giggs scored against Tottenham, just before half-time.

'What a great left boot!'

'Right into the right side of the net – that goalie didn't stand a chance!'

Kelly flew through the front door from school, flung her bag down and immediately reached for her *Match of the Day* video footage. Maths homework could definitely wait.

Carol called from the kitchen. 'Kelly, what sauce do you want with your fish and chips?'

No answer.

'Kelly? Kelly? You're not watching that Giggs *again*, are you?'

Carol watched as her daughter ran and balanced a ball in front of the sofa flipping it this way and that while studying the young player on the screen, watching his every move.

By the time Bernard came back from work in the evening, she was still there.

'Dad! Dad! Did you see that turn he did just then? It's amazing. I wanna turn like that!'

She watched again transfixed, as he darted and danced around defenders. He made it look so easy as he headed for the goal. Kelly threw the ball up into the air again, as she aimed to copy the turn.

'What a great touch too, Dad! First time!'

'Kelly – mind that vase!' Another precious ornament in the Smith household was smashed to smithereens.

'Whoops!' said Kelly, 'Sorry, Mum. I think I've mastered that turn though.'

'You'll have to practise with a soft ball in here, Kelly, we can't have yet another breakage.'

Bernard couldn't fault their daughter's dedication or enthusiasm, though, as he bent down to sweep up the pieces. She was so excited.

Kelly's eyes shone. 'I wanna be him, Dad. I wanna be Ryan. That's how I wanna play. I wanna make defenders not wanna be defenders anymore. What did Alex Ferguson say? Ryan scares them so bad he gives them twisted blood!'

'Oh yeah?'

'Yeah, and I don't reckon me and Ryan are that different anyway. We both do a killer left foot, he's a winger like me, we're both fast, we can both dribble and I can out-run players too, Dad! And I always know when a good cross is going to happen! Just like him! It's an instinct! And he knows just when to score on target.'

Bernard looked up and smiled.

'I'm sorry Kell, I'm sorry there aren't any women footballers for you to look up to.'

'Why is that, Dad? Why are the best footballers blokes? In fact, why aren't there any professional women footballers at all?'

Bernard sighed. 'Good question, can't answer it.'

Kelly looked at him and said: 'I'm just gonna have to be the female Ryan Giggs, then, aren't I?'

'Nah', he replied. 'You'll be Kelly Smith – a player in your own right, who'll inspire lots of girls to play football.'

'Thanks, Dad.'

CHAPTER 7

WATFORD LADIES

Kelly had made up her mind – she wasn't going to play with boys again. She'd just had enough of the grief she got. Her dad had other ideas though, and didn't want her to give up.

'Get in the car, Kelly, we're going to Watford Ladies,' he said with a wink. 'Now I know it's not Watford FC, but it's the next best thing...'

'Yeah, Watford FC, that's who my mate Paul will get to play for I bet, not fair.'

'I know.'

Kelly looked around the training facilities at Watford Ladies, based at Kings Langley FC. There were no proper changing rooms for girls, but she was used to that.

'Come and meet the team you could be playing with!' said Bernard enthusiastically.

Kelly wasn't quite sure where to look as she walked along the grounds towards four women. Her shyness kicked in, as well as her disappointment that there were only four of them.

'Flipping five-a-side,' she thought to herself. 'Why can't I play ten-a-side?'

She hissed under her breath. 'Dad, they're all enormous!'

'Bit harsh, Kelly!' They're just bigger than you, that's all.'

Kelly was introduced to them. They were friendly but all seemed to loom over her, in both height and width. She couldn't believe she'd be playing alongside them.

'Hello Kelly!' A smiley-faced woman stretched her hand out to her. 'I'm Susan. We've all heard you're a bit of a wonder kid! Lucky to have you on our team, eh?'

It seemed rude to ask how old they all were but she assumed the youngest was eighteen. The eldest was thirty-five, though they were all ancient as far as she was concerned.

'They've got lots of experience, Kelly, they'll help you improve your skills,' her dad said.

Kelly was excited to play with other girls for the first time... well, with other women in this case. But she was frustrated at their first away game in Ipswich.

'Ummm... have you seen that dwarf they've got playing?' she heard one of the opponents scoff.

'Yep, this should be easy then!'

'I'll show 'em,' thought Kelly, 'as soon as I get running out and attacking.'

But it didn't quite work out like that.

'We're gonna have to put you in goal, Kelly,' said Susan. Kelly's face fell.

'Sorry,' Susan went on, 'we just don't want you to get pulverised out there.' Kelly didn't feel strong enough to argue, but she wanted to be out on the pitch running around, attacking, scoring goals.

For the first forty-five minutes of the game Kelly worked her socks off and did her best to defend her goal for the team.

'Great save, Kelly!!' She heard her team mates roar each time. 'Amazing!'

Kelly got more and more confident. Each time an attacker got too close, she got better at anticipating which foot they were going to use and where they were aiming to plant the goal.

She didn't let up and only conceded one goal that day. Although they lost 1–0 she was proud of the result, as were her teammates.

'If you can do that in goal Kelly, maybe we should have let you on the pitch!'

'Great things come in small packages, eh?!' said one Ipswich opponent who walloped her on the back as she ran past.

Kelly smiled. This wasn't so bad.

Not long after that, a girl her own age called Debbie Garvey joined. She was a formidable striker. She and Kelly became an unstoppable pair, assisting and shooting goals. They had a good instinct for where each other were on the pitch. One night in the car on the way back from training, Bernard asked them both how they were getting on with Watford Ladies. 'Yeah, alright,' replied Debbie, 'we just wish there were more girls our own age.'

'And I wish we had better facilities,' said Kelly, 'they were even better at Garston, Dad!'

'Well,' said Bernard, 'I've been chatting to a guy called Norman Burns, great bloke, it seems he really wants to get more girls into football.'

Kelly's ears pricked up.

'He's heard how good you both are... he wants you both to join.'

Watford Ladies weren't too happy to lose two of their best strikers but were happy that Kelly and Debbie were able to play with girls their own age.

They wished them both well. 'Just make sure you make it to Wembley.'

'Yeah,' said Kelly, 'maybe in a few years!' Little did she know then, it was to be earlier than expected.

*

Pinner Park drew girls from all over London, not just

Watford. Kelly and Debbie loved their new team.

But in particular, they appreciated Norman Burns' support and encouragement. He believed that girls could play football just as well as boys and was prepared to give them a chance to develop their skills. Under his coaching they became one of the best teams around, and played eleven-a-side as well as five-a-side. Kelly still loved playing midfield and continued to perfect her touches and dribbling.

They were so good that they got to play in a final against Arsenal at Wembley Arena. This was a five-a-side match, organised by the Metropolitan Police. Bernard watched with pride. He could see her performance was improving all the time. She seemed faster than ever, speeding through people, dribbling through people's legs and keeping control of the ball, even between the thickest of defence structures.

'It's like she's jumping between raindrops,' commented John Jones, the manager of Wembley Ladies. John watched as Kelly slalomed through between two defenders to score the winning goal that saw the team lift the trophy, presented by former England goalkeeper Ray Clemence.

John approached Kelly after the match. 'You've got a great left foot on you,' he said to her. She was still getting her breath back.

'And right!' shouted one of her teammates. Kelly went a bit bashful – she felt awkward when her talents were praised and always hoped her moves on the pitch said enough.

John was surprised by how shy she was. She seemed to have no mercy out there against opponents but here, in conversation, she seemed a lot quieter in comparison.

'Who's your dream team to play for, Kelly?'

Without a second's thought she replied:

'Arsenal.'

'How'd you like to join Wembley Ladies in the meantime?' he asked. 'You're definitely good enough. We just might need to work on making that right foot as tough as the left.' He smiled. 'And it's still a London team.'

'Um, I'm not sure... I...' Kelly looked around for

her dad, who was soon at her side. She liked to run
these decisions past him first, so she could collect her
thoughts and ask for his advice. The car trip home
was always a good time for that.

'I've got to sit my GCSEs next year...'

Bernard said: 'She's still only fifteen, John.'

'Well okay, no pressure, but perhaps you'd like to
just join the reserves?'

Kelly's eyes lit up. Deep down, she knew that
football was all she wanted to do, but she was feeling
the stress of next year. She did feel torn between
doing what she loved but wanted a back-up plan
too. If she was in the reserves, she could keep one
foot in. It was frustrating – she knew that a teenage
boy would just jump at the chance, but she knew
there weren't the same professional opportunities for
women down the line. But Wembley Ladies were a
good side, and she knew they had a great reputation.

Kelly turned sixteen towards the end of 1994.
The Football Association had finally taken on the
women's national league and renamed it the FA
Women's Premier League. This already sounded

more serious to Kelly. And Wembley Ladies were in the top division of the three levels, with ten teams in each one. It still wasn't enough, though. She knew a life of riches and wealth didn't lie ahead of her either, as it did for the likes of Ian Wright, who lived in mansions on Sandbanks or drove Ferraris. It may have had 'premier' in the title, but it wasn't all that 'premier' in reality.

In the car home Kelly was silent until she said: 'I wish there were more professional opportunities, Dad. Why's it still so amateur? I've just got to fit it in and around my studies and spare time.'

'I know Kell... it's not fair. And I'll tell you what else isn't fair, the fee I need to pay for you to play at the start of each season – for the referees and pitches.'

Kelly sighed.

'But it's worth it, Kelly. I see how much joy you get from playing, you can tell it's your one love. It's absolutely worth every penny.'

Everyone seemed to confirm what Kelly suspected. She needed a backup plan. And this was reiterated by her careers adviser who immediately looked dubious when she mentioned football as a career. Kelly sat opposite the adviser, knowing there was little point going on about how much she loved football. So she'd make the next fifteen minutes easier for her.

'I'm thinking about the Army,' she said. 'Or.. maybe firefighting? Or I could become a police officer...'

'I hear you're an incredible athlete. Have you thought about training to be a PE teacher?'

Kelly knew this one was coming, but she had in all honesty considered it herself. She was relieved to leave the dreaded maths lessons behind her, after her GCSEs, and concentrate on what she really enjoyed – physical education.

'We're really proud of you, Kelly,' said Carol, as her daughter started her new BTEC National Diploma in Sports Science at West Herts College in Watford. So she might not be able to carve out a glamorous or well paid football career, not just yet anyway. But so what? She would still get to study an interesting qualification and still play football, even if only on the side.

CHAPTER 8

AMERICAN DREAM AND WEMBLEY DEBUT

'Don't worry, Kelly,' said Bernard, 'you're gonna do great.' Kelly was representing Pinner Park at the Watford Football Festival and her dad could tell she was nervous.

Kelly was quite intimidated as it was the first tournament playing against international teams from countries such as the USA, Denmark, Germany and Sweden. But she knew her team were good enough. They'd made it to the final. She looked for Bernard, who was on the touchline watching his daughter play proudly. He struck up conversation with another spectator, Terry Undercoffer. He said: 'That player from Pinner, she's got a real special talent.' Bernard was used to his daughter receiving praise. But little did he know he was scouting for the States.

Kelly couldn't believe it when Terry called her the next day.

'How'd you like a scholarship to America?'

'Er, what?'

Terry and Kelly met. As Kelly drank her milkshake, it all sounded like a dream. He listed the pros – education, housing, but ultimately, the prospect of being paid to do what she loved: play football. She wondered if she had a sugar rush from her drink as she took it all in. She'd be training full time – not just Tuesday and Thursday evenings.

Kelly's parents were delighted to hear her news but had reservations too. America was not a hop and a skip away for their daughter – it was all across the Atlantic.

But it was also an opportunity that her father, in particular, had begun to prepare himself for: his little girl going to the US. He'd sort of always prepared himself for it. Because he knew it was the best thing for her.

Kelly sighed. 'I just wish I could do this in Watford, Dad. Or even just England.'

'You're good enough to take your time, Kelly.'

'But opportunities like this don't come around that often, Dad.'

Kelly talked it over with American coach Betty Ann Kempf. Betty agreed that Kelly needed a Plan B, and her advice was reassuring:

'Hey, there's no rush. Keep studying, we're still going to want you in a year's time, your talent won't disappear.'

Kelly was relieved and happy they had such faith in her. In her heart, it didn't feel quite feel right to go to America at that time, so she settled back down to studying.

*

The girls sat in the changing rooms before the FA Cup match, trying not to let their fear show. It was Kelly's senior debut for Wembley Ladies in Wembley Stadium and, although she couldn't wait to get on the pitch, she was nervous. They were just about to play the Doncaster Belles who had a fierce reputation for being pretty much unbeatable. The Doncaster Belles also had two experienced seasoned England players on their team – centre- forward Karen Walker, and midfielder Gillian Coultard who dominated the field and had contributed greatly to the team's success since joining at the age of thirteen. Wembley Ladies were right to be nervous.

Kelly focused on John's sterling pep talk.

'Now listen, girls, I know they've got a good reputation but don't let them intimidate you, you're just as good as them.'

'They all say we haven't got a prayer!' piped up one.

'No-one ever beats them, John!' said another.

'But does that mean they can't ever be beaten? Listen to me, everyone is talking about what a strong side you are – they may have the experience but you're brave and creative! We may not beat them tonight, but you're not going to give them an easy time or concede too easily – I just know it.'

He added: 'Go and show them what you can do. And you're on home turf! So go and win this first leg!'

As Kelly ran out and saw the blur of the opponents' blue-and-yellow strip she picked out her dad in the crowd and immediately felt calmer. She always did when she spotted him. She reminded herself of her favourite mantra: 'Always play with a smile on your face.' Whatever happened, she'd got this far, an FA Cup game at Wembley playing the game she loved. And like John said, she could be playing for England one day, just like Coultard and Walker.

Out on the pitch, her fears melted away and she forgot she was playing against more experienced people. She could feel an energy between them all that gave her the faith to play her best. She stayed patient knowing she was building up to do something special. Just before half-time, it was 2–1 to the Belles. Kelly dropped deep to pick up the ball in the midfield, with her back to goal, and turned brilliantly to create space and pass it on. Without waiting, she took off towards the penalty box with speed, ready to pick it up again. She caught a perfectly weighted return ball with her first touch and dribbled her way through the Belles' defence, which separated for her with surprise and puzzlement. Finally, she turned, she saw a space open up for her, and went for the right side of the net with her left boot – GOAL!!!!! She'd just scored her first senior goal.

The match ended in a 3–3 draw but, just as John had predicted, the Wembley Ladies had not made it easy for the Belles. Normally, they thrashed the other side easily. After the match, Coultard smacked Kelly on the back and said, 'You'll be playing for England in no time.' Kelly was still only sixteen and didn't dare to think her talent could be recognised this quickly. But sure enough, the following year, just a few days after her seventeenth birthday she was playing for England against Italy at Roker Park, home of Sutherland AFC, for a European Championship qualification match.

'I can't believe it!' She kept saying to herself over and over. She was barely seventeen and already one of her girlhood dreams had come true – 'I'm playing for England!'

'Listen,' said her coach Ted Copeland, 'you'll be up against experience in this match but just play as you always do. Don't think about the fact you're in the England team now or that you're up against international players.'

One of these particularly experienced players was midfielder Hope Powell, who Kelly knew had nearly sixty caps to her name. She was a little intimidated to be on the pitch with such a legend but found her friendly, with an upbeat yet calming aura about her. Kelly felt immediately put at ease, as though she'd always known her.

Hope smiled and said: 'I was about your age when I made my England debut. You're going to be great.'

One to look out for on the Italian team who Kelly found especially impressive was striker Carolina Morace who, again, had plenty of experience. It was a freezing cold night as Kelly jogged out on to the pitch but the pride, excitement and adrenaline soon warmed her up. They were still playing in men's football shirts but there were three lions on the shirt nonetheless – she scanned the stadium to find her dad as she always did and could see he was welling up.

Kelly concentrated on running up and down the left wing, doing her best to assist and get crosses to Marianne Spacey and Karen Walker, who were playing up front. It was good to have Karen on her side for a change and not be fighting her. Karen was at least ten years older than Kelly, and the teenager appreciated the experience her older teammate brought to the game. Marianne, meanwhile, was a feared forward who managed to score from twenty yards down the pitch.

Kelly didn't score but she knew she'd contributed to their 1–1 draw. Her confidence was building and she knew it was only a matter of time before she was slamming goals into the back of the net for her country.

Her time came only a few weeks later. Her deadly left foot came through again, as she deftly created some space for herself and caught a shot beautifully with her second touch to score her first goal for

England, in a 5–0 win against Croatia at Charlton Athletic.

Playing for England gave Kelly fantastic opportunities to develop her international footing. But something didn't quite fit right with her on her local team.

Bernard could see something was on her mind when he picked her up after practice at Wembley Ladies.

'I don't get it, you're doing what you love, you're only seventeen and you've scored for England!'

'I know, Dad, that's great, of course it is... I'm just getting frustrated.'

'You get on with John, don't you?'

'Yeah, he's a great coach, in many ways. But he focuses on fitness too much. I just want to get better on the ball, improve my technicality and work out how to score goals – that's the important thing!'

'Where do you want to go?'

Kelly knew, deep down, but she didn't dare say.

CHAPTER 9

KELLY'S DREAM TEAM

Kelly had to pinch herself as she wandered around the Highbury Stadium with Vic Akers, the Arsenal Ladies' manager. The stands were all empty, but she could almost hear the crowds cheering again and see the fans waving their red scarves, just as she had done six years back when she went to her first game. Back then, she'd worn their yellow JVC strip and dreamt she might wear it for real one day. Now, here she was, wandering around the stadium's plush and famous marble halls, about to sign for the team.

Vic even showed her the palatial dressing rooms with heated floors. Kelly could feel the history of all the great games and players, as she saw a line of trophies from the glory days.

Vic Akers smiled and said: 'Football's answer to the Taj Mahal.'

They headed outside to watch the team train. Kelly saw a big beefy man in Arsenal kit approaching them. 'Oh my god,' she thought, 'it's Martin Keown – just as enormous in the flesh!' It was surreal to see him up close, rather than a mere dot running around on the pitch. Outside, she saw a man in a raincoat talking to the coach Pat Rice. She recognised him as Arsène Wenger.

'He's going to do great things for the team', said Vic.

Kelly hardly needed Arsenal Ladies to be sold to her. She was honoured to be asked to play for the club. Vic had been interested in the young star for a while, but had not wanted to approach her until he heard she was unhappy at Wembley Ladies.

'Really?' said Kelly. 'In all honesty, I always hoped I'd be approached by Arsenal. I've supported them since I was a kid!'

'Who's your favourite Arsenal player?'

'Ian Wright', she replied like a shot.

As Kelly went to leave, Vic handed her a pair of black boots. 'Here you go, have these, they're Ian's.'

This really was the icing on the cake. How could she turn Arsenal Ladies down now?!

*

Kelly flew with ferocity down the pitch at Highbury. She was playing in the Premier League Final against Liverpool. One of their defenders was hot on her heels trying to close her down. But no-one could get near her as she stuck one in the top corner for the first goal of the match, well within the first twenty minutes. Just before half-time Kelly saw another opportunity open up, and she booted in her second, just like Giggsy. There was an almost jubilant atmosphere among the team at half-time but they were determined not to concede any goals that day, and Vic warned them not to get complacent.

'Don't think you've got it all bagged up just yet. Their attackers are still looking pretty strong to me. Keep it up and don't concede!'

About thirty minutes into the second half Kelly

passed a nifty ball to help create one of their goals. At full time, Arsenal Ladies lifted the trophy – they'd won the league 3–0 against Liverpool. The team were ecstatic and Kelly knew her reputation as a formidable force on the pitch was well and truly cemented.

The game was tinged with sadness, though. Kelly's BTEC studies were over and she'd achieved the grades she needed, so her move to the USA was imminent, to the disappointment of both her and Vic. As much as she loved playing for Arsenal Ladies, she now had a chance to play professionally.

'We'll miss you Kelly,' said Vic, 'but you know, there's always a place for you back here, if it doesn't work out.' He couldn't hide his disappointment as he said goodbye.

'I know Vic, thanks so much for all you've done for me.'

Kelly was going to miss Arsenal Ladies, particularly Vic, who believed in her, and supported her. Already, before the age of twenty, she'd achieved some of her biggest lifetime goals – playing for Arsenal and her country. She was firmly established in the England team and by the summer of 1997 she had four goals to her name from 14 appearances. But she really wanted it to work out in the USA, to be on the ball every day, to make the switch from amateur to professional and develop her skills. She still couldn't do that at home.

Kelly had been given a few options in the USA – three American colleges had showed an interest. But Kelly picked Seton Hall in New Jersey and signed a three-year scholarship with the Seton Hall Pirates. The USA beckoned.

After they had taken Kelly to the airport, Bernard and Carol arrived home. Bernard shut the front door of their house behind him and looked at Carol. Already the place felt empty without their daughter. It was about four in the afternoon, a Saturday. Ordinarily, they'd hear the sound of a ball bouncing against the wall outside, music from Kelly's room or her shouting at the TV if Arsenal was playing.

They walked to the park to take the dog out. All around, people were out enjoying their weekends,

t
E
h

w
tl

S
d

w
f

e
f(

f(

h

a
S
g
V
b
i
h
t
S
g

she knew
and felt th
the opposi
to score.

It was t
Dame ha(
Kelly war
momentu
in midfiel
easily pas
block her
past them
net – GO

The Pi
about Ke
the team
level at 2
In extra t
teammat
jumped a
looked o
confiden

'Thanks for persuading me to stay, Mum.'

Bernard got on the line.

'We got the picture of you in the local newspaper! Turning into a right celebrity out there, aren't you?!'

'Well, maybe, Dad... funny, isn't it? I never made it to the local paper in Watford, did I?!'

'You will, Kelly. You'll make it to the nationals, in fact!'

The recognition was still a bit strange to her, though. She noticed people looking at her in the street, whispering or throwing admiring glances. She saw her picture headlined with: 'Easy on the eye, as well as easy on the ball.'

Maybe she just wasn't used to it. But something told her she'd have to get used to it. Her tummy fluttered a little. Why did that thought frighten her? Ultimately, she just loved scoring goals.

CHAPTER 11

RUNNING FROM PUBLIC SPEAKING

Kelly just got better and better as the season went on. And she knew she was feared. Teams were marking her more heavily than ever before but this all helped her to vary and develop her style. By her third season she'd scored six hat tricks.

Her attacking skills were recognised with NCAA Offensive Player of the Year. Betty Ann continued to build the team around Kelly's abilities, with support from goalkeeper Stacey Nagle and midfielder Courtney Wood.

'I can see how you've helped everyone else improve,' said Betty Ann.

Before their game against Pittsburgh the girls were excited to find out the match was going to be televised live. This was the most commercial attention The Pirates had ever received. After the match, reporters swarmed around Kelly. She'd scored four goals to achieve a 4–1 win. But she just wanted to celebrate with the rest of the team.

At the Big East Awards dinner, Kate Markgraf made an acceptance speech when she received her award for Defensive Player of the Year. Kelly was listening, admiring how utterly at ease Kate seemed to be with the attention focused on her. But suddenly, a terrifying thought hit Kelly: she would have to do the same thing when she picked up her Offensive Player of the Year Award. Her stomach churned and she felt her hands begin to sweat. There was a pounding feeling in her head.

She sneaked out, as quickly and as silently as she could, to the toilets. She just didn't feel she had anything to say that counted. And she didn't know how to say it. And even if she could get the words out, would she go red and start stuttering? She felt ashamed that she was hiding in there, missing out on this event where everyone had gathered, in part, to see and hear her. In that moment, she wished she was back home, with her dad watching a match, and no eyes on her. The pressure of expectations felt too much and she burst into tears.

Betty Ann appeared in the doorway.

'Ah, there you are!' She came over and gave her a big hug.

'I don't want to do it!'

'It's alright, Kelly, you don't have to do anything you don't want. No-one's gonna make you.'

*

Kelly had finished her qualifications to teach Physical Education and was considering her options. Should she head back to England?

Betty Ann, though, was keen she stayed on and suggested she took the job of assistant football coach at Seton Hall:

'I think you'd be great.' She also thought it would improve Kelly's confidence in speaking to people.

There was another reason for Kelly to stay too.

There was talk of creating a professional league – the new Women's United Soccer Association League.

As Kelly was aware, English women's football was still very much behind on that front. As much as she missed Vic, the Arsenal Ladies and everyone back at home, she knew in her heart that her home country was a long way off from embracing women's football as a professional sport.

As Kelly watched the uproarious reaction of the USA to its team winning the Women's World Cup in 1999 this was compounded even more. Over 90,000 fans watched the USA defeat China in the final. Big names such as Bobby Charlton and Jurgen Klinsmann discussed the best players from the tournament – Mia Hamm was the star of the game that year and became Nike's third-highest paid athlete behind Michael Jordan and Tiger Woods. Kelly just wished she could have played in that game, but England had failed to qualify.

Not long after, the Women's United Soccer Association League was created for the 2001 season. Kelly, the sole representative from England in the entire league, began playing for the Philadelphia Charge team, based close to New Jersey.

Kelly talked excitedly to her dad on the phone. 'There were thirty or forty international players to choose from and I was picked second!'

'Who's the coach?'

'Mark Krikorian.'

'He must know what he's doing.'

'I really don't want to let him down. Some sports journalist said he's made "a bonehead move".'

'Just ignore that, Kelly, I'm afraid to say it's because you're English. England's women's football just still doesn't have a good reputation on the international scene. But everyone's who seen you play here knows how good you are.'

'I know, Dad. It's not fair I'm judged for that, though.'

'Don't let it hurt you. Focus on this next opportunity. And remember, you're playing professional football now in a professional league! Look at how far you've come!'

'Thanks, Dad. I can't wait for it to start! It's going

to be strange singing "The Star Spangled Banner", though...'

*

Kelly was now part of the Philadelphia Charge side, and was overwhelmed by the huge support for the team before their match against San Diego. Between 10,000 and 12,000 people all showed up before the game in their red and white Philadelphia shirts.

Surrounded by love and support, Kelly felt tears welling up as she stood on the pitch. Okay, so she wasn't playing for her country, but she was in a professional league. She couldn't keep her tears back as she stood there singing. As the fireworks went off after the American national anthem she thought: 'Wow – my dream has come true.'

And what a buzz to play in front of a sell-out crowd! This was such a contrast to playing for England where she felt the crowds of spectators weren't really there to see them – like the lesser-known support act before the headliner at a festival. She might play with an England shirt on her back, but no-one in her country knew her name.

Kelly set out to prove her naysayers wrong –
those journalists who had called picking her a
'bonehead move' in the national press. She scored
a penalty kick in the first half but was constantly
looking for opportunities to run and attack in her
forward position. But her breakthrough came with a
long range kick. She picked up a ball from defender
Heather Mitts and hit it from twenty yards with
a left boot specialty – GOAL! All live on TV. She
wished her dad was actually there to see her score
her first professional goal, but her coach's beaming
face and the joy of her teammates was enough.
At the end of the week she picked up the 'Most
Valuable Player' award.

'What a way to start, Kelly!' said Bernard. 'We're
so proud!'

'I feel like a celebrity here, Dad.'

'You will be over here one day, Kelly.'

'I'm not holding my breath, Dad...'

Luckily, back in the UK, former player Hope
Powell was now coaching the England team

and beginning to turn their fortunes around. In
2001, Kelly played for England in the European
Championship in Germany. The tournament clashed
with her commitments in the USA but playing for
her country came first. The team drew against the
Russians but were well beaten by two strong sides –
Sweden and Germany. Still, at least they'd qualified
under Hope.

CHAPTER 12

KELLY THE COACH

Kelly was working on a demanding training schedule with the strength and conditioning coach Duane Carlisle. She'd suffered a sprained ankle injury but they also worked on her goals for the game.

'What do you want to be, Kelly?' Duane asked her.

'One of the best players in the world.'

'One of the best?'

'Okay,' she conceded with a smile. 'The best.'

'You can be, Kelly – you're fast, but you can be faster. And you're strong, but you can be stronger.'

'I love running at players, Duane – always have done. I want them to be scared when I run at them – one on one!'

'Well, let's get to work!'

Mark called Kelly in for a chat.

'We've got a new striker – Marinette Pichon.' said Mark.

'Wow, she's brilliant!' said Kelly, who had watched her in action in other games. This position change also meant Kelly was moved from a forward role to midfield where she could attack in the centre.

'Thanks Mark! My ankles could do with a rest!' Up front, she got fouled a lot and was still recovering from her injury.

'I've got some other news too', said Mark. 'We want you to be captain of the team.'

'What? But wow, thanks Mark.'

'You're showing such great strength of character, Kelly, I've really seen you grow. You didn't let that ankle injury get to you – you just worked on getting better. I really trust you to lead a team, Kelly.'

'It's a missile!' was how Atlanta Beat's Tom Stone, the opposition coach, described Kelly's neat and powerful free kick in their opening campaign match.

'How are we doing, Kelly?' the players asked their captain at half-time.

'Great, but we need to open it up on the wings a bit, guys, and keep an eye out for that defender trying to close you down.'

The team listened attentively to Kelly and she began to enjoy coaching. It didn't feel as scary as public speaking to her, Her playing was improving too – she scored four goals and three assists in her first seven games of the season.

*

One day, Kelly was playing in a match against Bay Area CyberRays. She knew Marinette was to her right – the pair had an instinctive feel for where each other was on the pitch. She turned her body in with her left foot to make the cross. At the same time, she heard a popping sound and felt instant pain in her knee.

'Aaaaaagh!!!' As she fell to the ground in pain she suspected it was an ACL injury – a tear in the middle ligament of the knee.

It was hard not to feel panic. Every footballer dreaded this and she knew it could put her out of the game for the season. The X-rays confirmed her worst fears.

'I can't believe it, Dad,' she cried down the phone, 'they're gonna have to do surgery!'

'I'm so sorry Kell. But remember, the surgeons know what they're doing, you'll feel like you've got a brand new knee in no time.'

'What if I can't play football ever again, Dad?!'

'Don't think that way Kelly – just concentrate on getting better.'

Kelly had to take one day at a time, which was utterly frustrating for her. She'd only ever been used to minor strains or muscle pulls but this was major. Surgery had gone well but now she was on crutches and knew recovery would take precious time – time away from playing football. For someone so active, this was hard.

Each night she had to sleep in a special machine that turned her knee gradually. She could only sleep on her back, but had always been used to sleeping on her side.

It was all getting on top of her. Missing football

and lack of sleep made the whole process seem even more insurmountable. Even watching comedy on TV did little to lift her spirits. She just wasn't built to sit on a sofa for too long and missed her active lifestyle.

She spent a lot of time on the phone to her parents.

'I'm so low, Dad.'

'Just keep that knee moving as much as you can, Kelly, and visualise being back out on that pitch again.'

She was already dreaming about scoring goals all the time, and they were the best dreams. When she woke up, she thought she was back in her old life for a split second, ready to leap up and go training. She worked on building up her quad muscle, hamstring and calf back up to the level she needed for professional sport.

One day, she made it out to watch the Philadelphia team training. They were ecstatic to see her:

'Kelly, we've missed you so much!'

As her teammates ran over to her, they could see how down she was and how much whiter in the face she looked. She'd missed them so much too and wished she could join in with them. She missed Marinette in particular. They had such a strong understanding on the pitch together.

'Just focus on getting better, Kelly!' said Marinette. 'It's not the same playing without you.'

Kelly could hardly smile back as she lay out on the treatment table in the rehabilitation room, struggling to move her leg.

At night she lay awake pondering the same question: 'When will this heal?' It felt like forever for her. She missed the buzz from playing and letting out the part of her personality that became so alive on the pitch.

She worked tirelessly with the medical staff. 'Will I be able to play again?' she occasionally asked them out of desperation.

'Kelly – of course you will!' they would reply. 'You were born to play football and it's our job to get you back to doing what you do best.'

On particularly bad days Kelly really appreciated the Americans for their upbeat positivity. But she needed a goal.

'Okay,' said the medical staff, 'when do you want to be back running?'

'When can I be?'

'When do you want to be?'

'As soon as possible!'

'Well, let's work on that then! You'll need to put in two to three extra hours of work a day I reckon. But you can do that – right?'

'Yes!'

Sure enough, she was running within five months. It was a step-by-step process, building up from straight runs into curved running. But it needed to be done to get back to playing football.

Support from the team really helped. She missed them, but knowing they missed her gave her the strength to push on and get better. She watched Philadelphia play a game from the sidelines and cheered on as Marinette scored an amazing goal. Straight after, she ran over to Kelly and lifted her shirt to show a vest underneath with her name and number on it – Smith 8. Kelly's eyes welled up with tears and she couldn't stop crying.

Her first day running back out on the pitch with the team elevated her spirits. She felt a new high she'd not experienced in a long time. She was running slowly but she was back doing what she loved with the girls.

'It's really helped me appreciate the small things, Dad,' she told Bernard. 'Just wearing the kit again and not being stuck in the changing room while they're out playing.'

'Don't rush it though, Kelly, please!'

'I won't, Dad.'

However, she only got to play one more game until another knee injury put her out for the rest of the season. It meant she missed qualifying matches for England too.

'All the work I've put in, Dad, it's not fair.'

'You've just got to be patient, Kelly.'

'I hate not playing, Dad. But not playing for England really hurts, I think I could have helped us qualify for the World Cup and made a difference there.'

'At least women's footie is becoming more high profile, Kelly, and I do think that's down to players like you.'

CHAPTER 13

DISASTER ON THE PITCH

In 2003, Kelly had more bad news. The Women's United Soccer Association folded due to financial issues. Kelly was in shock that her whole professional dreams had been taken away.

The best option was to move across to the Women's League, but this was still only semi-professional.

As ever, she went to her dad for advice, who suggested she should come back to England.

'Dad, I want to stay, I believe in football here, they take it seriously. All the best players are here.'

Kelly joined the New Jersey Wildcats along with Marinette. She was another reason for Kelly to stay in the USA. Their friendship off the pitch was just as solid as it was on. They worked hard, but the magic between them came naturally.

Kelly was just beginning to get back into her stride when disaster struck on the pitch during a game between the Wildcats and Delaware. She knew they were aggressive opponents and, as one of the most feared players, Kelly was used to unfair tackles. She sensed a defender behind her as she received the ball and took a touch on her left foot. Suddenly, she felt excruciating pain in her right leg.

She jumped up in the air screaming and fell back down in agony. She knew her leg was broken. She hopped to the sidelines in shock at the malicious intent behind the tackle.

At the hospital, her teammates gathered around her bed as she cried tears of frustration and disbelief. Kelly faced more endless months of rehabilitation stretched out in front of her – just lying on a sofa and not playing. It all seemed so stupid! And for what? A completely pointless move from an opponent who didn't deserve to be called a player.

But this was Kelly's longest endurance test without football and it plunged her into a deep depression. Close friends like Marinette couldn't reach her.

She tried hard to keep how low she was from her parents. She didn't want them to know because she didn't want to be a burden. She was in it for the long haul, facing this one alone.

Her enthusiasm for anything else in life vanished. Everything seemed grey as she spent long days and nights propped up on the sofa, watching the seasons change and pass. But nothing seemed to change for her. Not even the first primroses of spring brought her any joy – nothing did without the buzz of doing what she knew she did best.

At night, she dreamt of jumping, leaping and dribbling around players – setting up goals and left-booting balls into the back of the net.

She watched the team from the sidelines and couldn't help but feel envy. She wished it was her flying down that pitch – 'I'd do this, I'd do that, I'd set that up!'

She was angry too. She'd been playing semiprofessionally when it happened – would it have happened if she'd been in a professional league and the play was refereed better?

But worse than that, deep within her there was a growing sense that she really was a nobody without football.

One night, she shared this fear with Marinette.

'That's not true!' she replied.

One night Kelly went home feeling particularly low. She looked around her for something, anything, that might take her mind away from it all, to distract her from her worries. There was nothing in her room that made her feel any different – football was all she was good at. What did she amount to, if she couldn't play? She threw herself onto her bed and let out a sob, followed by another one. And then something stopped her – the thought of her parents' faces. She took a few deep breaths, until she felt calm again, and picked up the phone.

She was so relieved when she heard her dad's steady voice on the end of the line. At the sound of his simple 'Hello' she burst into tears straight away.

'That's it, I'm coming to get you,' Bernard said. He flew out on the next available flight and brought her home. It was a relief to be rescued and she managed a smile as they saw a 'God Bless America' sticker on the bumper of someone's car.

She turned to her dad. 'I'm done with this country, Dad. I'm never going back.'

*

But returning to England didn't magically solve Kelly's problems of self-doubt. She didn't even know how she felt about football anymore.

'Hi Kelly, how are you?'

It was Vic Akers on the end of the line.

'Hmm... been better, Vic.'

'Well, it's great to know you're back, Kelly!'

'Look Vic, if you're phoning to try and get me to play football again, I'm just not there yet.'

Kelly knew she needed time to think and recover. She didn't feel positive about football yet, it had too many negative connotations attached to it.

Hope Powell knew not to push her either.

'Whatever happens, Kelly,' she said, 'I just want

you to get yourself back. Forget about football for now. Even if you never play again, let's work towards you feeling better about yourself.'

Kelly really appreciated that. Pressure was the last thing she needed right now.

'Thanks, Hope.'

'It is okay to talk you know, I'm always here at the end of the phone.'

Pippa Bennett, the England team doctor was a great emotional support too. Kelly began to discover she felt happier if she took just one day at a time and dealt with her feelings and emotions in the moment. It helped to talk to people too. She realised that she didn't have to go through all this alone and that people genuinely cared about her.

She shared a lot with Hope. 'I feel bad I don't want to play football, like I'm letting people down.'

'Give yourself time,' Hope replied, 'don't worry about what others want from you. You're the most important person now. Once you get your spirit back, then figure out if you want to play football or not.'

Eventually, Vic persuaded her to watch Arsenal

Ladies train. Kelly found she enjoyed it and wanted
to get out there with them. After only a month she
went to talk to Vic about re-signing with the team.
She also got to know new faces like Faye White, who
worked in the office at the men's training ground, as
well as playing for the club.

'We'd be so happy to have you back at the
Gunners, and very lucky too,' said Vic, smiling.

'Okay...' said Kelly, 'on one condition.'.

'Yes?'

'Is the Number Eight shirt available?'

'It's yours.'

Kelly had wanted to wear that shirt since she first
saw Ian Wright play at Highbury.

Her love for the game was slowly returning
and she realised her days in football were far from
over. In fact, she felt as though they were only just
beginning again.

CHAPTER 14

ARSENAL LADIES' FA CUPS

It was the FA Cup Final 2007 – Arsenal Ladies against Charlton Ladies at Nottingham Forest City Ground. Vic Akers gathered the team together before the match. 'Now, ladies... Arsène made the men's team "The Invincibles" back in 2003... Now we're going to claim that title for the women's team today.'

'Yes!!!' they all shouted back in agreement.

Just like when she was a little girl, Kelly always set new targets to beat and loved being on a team like Arsenal Ladies that felt the same. They had many talented players from the England team playing – like forward Rachel Yankey, midfielder Katie Chapman and England legend Faye White, who provided the backbone of the team. Kelly knew they could all walk out onto the pitch with confidence in their redcurrant Arsenal anniversary kit.

It was a Bank Holiday Monday so the crowds were huge – there was a record attendance of 24,529 and no rain.

They had a confidence about them as they smiled up at the sun shining brightly. Not only had they got technically better, their mentality was strong too – Kelly felt they'd win. And it was great to know they had huge crowds who wanted them to win too – it was easily the most watched game of women's club football so far.

Charlton's striker Eniola Aluko got the first goal in early to take the lead. Kelly felt some tension within the team, but she knew if they stayed patient and kept defending this well she could soon have a chance.

That chance came quicker than she anticipated. Only five minutes later, Kelly had the right-back Maria Bertelli hot on her heels to the left of the midfield. She'd been chasing her early. Smith kept control of the ball and saw she had a way to go past Charlton's defenders. There was another one just about to join Bertelli. In a split-second decision, Kelly booted it. The ball had a twenty-five-yard distance to travel and she'd given it just the right amount of spin to curl – she watched with relief as it soared above the defenders, then eased its way into the right side of the net – GOAL!

Kelly had judged it perfectly. Her teammates jumped around her with joy as they equalised. Eight minutes later there was more rejoicing as Jayne Ludlow got the ball in at the post after striker Lianne Sanderson's free kick. Arsenal were in the lead. Both Ludlow and Smith went on to score again in the second half, making the final score 4–1.

At the end of the game, Kelly ran over to hug Hope. She knew she couldn't have achieved this without her.

That season Vic and the team celebrated the club's twentieth anniversary with the unprecedented quadruple win of Premier League, UEFA Cup,

League Cup and FA Cup titles. They had easily achieved the title of 'The Invincibles'!

*

The following year, 2008, Arsenal Ladies faced Leeds United Ladies in the next FA Cup Final. As Kelly walked out she sensed this was the last time they would all play together and she realised how much she was going to miss it.

'I need to drink in every moment', she thought to herself.

She looked to Julie Fleeting, their target up front, who always knew the right position to be in. Next she looked to Karen Carney and Rachel Yankey, their incredible wingers, then Katie Chapman who closed down any wandering defence in the centre midfield. Kelly never felt the pressure was entirely all on her to score – if they missed the early goals they had enough talent that was willing to take chances.

They reached half-time and there was still no score. They were starting to flag under the pressure of Leeds, but they know they just needed to be patient.

Relief came a few minutes into the second half. Rachel ran up on the side to dribble past some defenders, and Kelly was then ready on the inside to receive the pass perfectly. She passed it back to Yankey before she started running to where she needed to be. Yankey passed to where she instinctively knew Kelly would run. Her boot met the ball at first contact and then boom – GOAL!

Kelly fell to the ground with relief. They were back in control of the tempo of the game.

After two more goals from Arsenal, Leeds scored for the first time. But Arsenal knew they were out of the danger zone. They went on to finish the game with a 4–1 win.

Kelly felt as though the whole team could burst with pride as they walked up to receive their medals. As she lifted the cup she saw Hope at the sidelines waving up to her. She had now scored five goals in three successive FA Women's Cup Finals. And a record 25,000 fans had watched the game.

As they celebrated, Vic called for all women's finals to be played at Wembley to reflect the growing interest and passion for the game. And Kelly knew the fun wasn't to end there – she'd soon be joining many of her teammates again to play for England. She couldn't wait.

CHAPTER 15

WOMEN'S WORLD CUP – 2007

'Come on!!!'

The England team couldn't contain their excitement as they walked out into the tunnel at the Stade de La Route de Lorient in France for their World Cup qualifying match. If they got through they'd be off to China, the hosting country. This was a big deal. The England team were playing well and had comfortably beaten all other countries in the qualifying games – Austria, Hungary and Holland. During the Holland game, Kelly had scored her second hat trick of the campaign. But the England Women's team hadn't beaten France since 1974, and they needed at least a draw to be sure of qualification – a tough ask.

The majority of the crowd were French, with only a small minority of England supporters cheering consistently throughout. The French crowd were silenced as England took the lead when Fara Williams scored a header. France drew in the eighty-eighth minute but when the final whistle blew the girls were ecstatic and ran over to the small group of England fans to thank them.

England had qualified to play for the Women's World Cup! The blur of the last few horrendous years seemed to clear before Kelly's eyes as they celebrated. It had all been worth it, all the hard work to get back to peak fitness for this dream to come true. She was playing again at the top of her game and loving every minute. And this time, she was going into the tournament without an injury. She couldn't wait for China.

Their World Cup match against Japan was one of their most important. Whoever won was likely to go through to play Germany at the quarter-finals. Germany was the team everyone was scared to compete against – they were playing well with their star player Birgit Prinz.

The night before the Japan game, Kelly lay on her hotel bed and tried to drown out the excited chitter-chatter of her teammates she could hear through the walls. She closed her eyes and worked on her visualisation techniques – playing out certain scenarios in her mind – Kaz passing to her, trusting where the ball was, imagining the feel of it at her feet before she belted it into the top of the net.

As they walked out into Hongkou Stadium brimming with excitement the England team were overwhelmed by the sheer size of the venue.

This is what it's all about, thought Kelly, as she scanned the crowds for her dad and family. She shook with pride as she sang the National Anthem, trying hard to get the words out past the bubble of pride in her throat.

Although confident, they knew Japan was a tough side with fantastic players like Aya Miyama who was particularly lethal with her free kicks. Eniola Aluko got the crowds excited when she nearly scored in the first half-hour but just missed the net. It helped add momentum to the game and put pressure on the goalkeeper. England were struggling to make a breakthrough but could feel their time coming if they were patient.

Then, the moment they were all dreading happened. Japan was granted a free kick after fifty-four minutes when Katie Chapman fouled a player. Miyama kicked it in easily. England's goalkeeper Rachel Brown didn't stand a chance. Japan were 1–0 up.

Things weren't looking good. Something had to turn around. Kelly could feel the tired energy within the team. Karen (Kaz) Carney got the ball and passed to Rachel Yankey who also had a narrow miss but just couldn't get the contact. Hope looked dejected from the sidelines but managed to smile.

There were just nine minutes remaining. Suddenly, Kaz was on the ball. Almost in desperation, she ran down the middle looking for a through, a pass, her feet frantically searching. Kelly knew she had some space and took a neat pass from Kaz along the ground. The defenders came towards her but she got through them, and tricked one of them into going where they didn't want to go with the Cruyff turn. Without thinking, she pirouetted on to her left foot to set up the direction for the ball.

She realised she still had contact with the ball, and a mere second later they'd have the ball off her. The goal was there, ready, waiting – there was space! She lifted her famous left boot and nailed the ball, into the bottom left hand corner of the net, well away from the keeper. GOAL!!

It felt as though Kelly's mind had gone blank for a moment but then the reality sunk in – she'd scored her first ever goal in the World Cup finals, just as the team needed it most.

The crowd went wild as, instinctively, Kelly took off her left boot and kissed it, taking it for a jog to the corner of the pitch. She wasn't sure whether to laugh, cry or burst. It had all built to this point. The England World Cup campaign was up and running again, thanks to her goal. England's best player had dazzled, just when the team had needed it most, and had dragged them out of a hole. The mood in the stadium shifted. The momentum was now with England.

Two minutes later, Kelly saw Fara Williams pick up the ball, and so she sped to get in the right spot. Williams passed it to Kelly, who had a chance to pass to Carney running down on the right side but decided to go it alone. Now Kelly was in the penalty spot. She had control of the ball. She beat one defender, two defenders and took a shot with her left foot. Quick as anything it bounced off the goalie and back at her. In a flash, she booted it back with her right foot – hard, it wasn't coming back this time! She knew she'd given it some force but she stared, almost in disbelief, as it went into the back of the net – GOAL!

Kelly stood for a second then yanked off her right boot as Rachel, Fara and Kaz jumped around and hugged her in euphoria – both boots had done the business and deserved congratulating! Heart-wrenchingly, Japan drew with another free kick, five minutes into injury time. Miyama was the free kick queen. England had been so close to winning 2–1 but now had to settle for a 2–2 draw. But nothing could take away from the elation of those two goals scored in Kelly's first ever World Cup. England were still in the running, thanks to her.

England's next opponents were Germany, the reigning European and World champions, a team packed full of world-class players. England were nervous but Hope's focus and hard work on defending had paid off and they held their own for a 0–0 draw. It was their best ever result against Germany. The England team were growing in confidence, thanks in part to Faye White's excellent defending and the threat of Kelly's boots.

The team were buzzing with even more confidence as they walked out into Chengdu Stadium in front of 30,730 spectators to face Argentina. This was one of their most enjoyable games – with the pressure of the last two behind them, the team felt ready to just have some fun on the pitch.

The first goal was an incredible long range shot from Casey Stoney, which Argentina's Eva Gonzáles knocked in for an own goal. Then it was Jill Stone's chance to shine with a goal from twenty yards. In the second half, Fara scored a penalty easily and the team, along with the jubilant crowd, knew that England were bound for the quarter-finals. González scored a free kick in the fiftieth minute but no-one was worried. Kelly Smith, the golden girl, tapped in their third goal from close range, after receiving a pass from Carney – her third of the tournament. Minutes later she went for a strike – cutting onto her favourite left foot from Rachel's pass. Finally, Kelly felt as though she was truly scaring those defenders – she smiled as she thought of the phrase 'twisted blood' again. England had beaten Argentina 6–1 and now faced the USA in the quarter-final.

Hope gathered them all together before they got on the coach. 'You have come so far. Whatever happens in the quarter-final, it was always my dream for us to get to this stage. I'm so proud of how you've all played. And most importantly, I've really seen your confidence grow.'

'Do you think we can do it, Kelly?' said Rachel.

'Yeah, course,' replied Kelly. But somehow, she wasn't sure. Technically, she believed their side were just as good as the USA but she also feared the opposing team were mentally strong. Her fears were justified: the USA beat them 3–0. It didn't help that they were missing their midfielder Faye White, who had been elbowed in the face in a previous match. England's World Cup dreams were over for 2007 but the team returned home proud. They were the only team to keep a clean sheet against Germany and take any points off the country. Next, it was time to look ahead to Euro 2009.

CHAPTER 16

FIFA AWARDS AND BOSTON BREAKERS

Back in England, Kelly was excited that the 2007
World Cup tournament had raised the profile of
women's football. Even if she'd wanted to hide from
the fame, she couldn't now. But over the years her
confidence in public speaking had really grown and
she wasn't so fazed by it, not even the teasing chat of
Jonathan Ross who asked her onto his show to talk
in front of millions.

More TV appearances followed: she went on *A
Question of Sport* with Matt Dawson and Kelly
Holmes, and *Gladiators*, where her quick feet helped
her out on many of the games – in particular, getting
the most foam balls into a pod. But best of all she

got to hang out with the host, who happened to be her idol Ian Wright. She was delighted when he praised her famous left boot and didn't even feel too embarrassed about it this time.

The accolades kept coming. One morning, watching Sky Sports News, Kelly happened to see her name flash up on the screen. She waited to see it scroll round again then screamed in excitement.

Her dad came running out. 'What? What??'

Her mum teased: 'You haven't broken another one of my vases have you?'

She turned to them both with tears in her eyes. 'I've been nominated for FIFA's Player of the Year!!!'

'Well, look at that!!! My little girl – one of the top five women footballers in the world!' said her dad. 'The best in my eyes.'

On the way to the FIFA Awards gala in Zürich, Kelly and her dad shared a limousine with football legend Pelé – Bernard was too frozen in awe to ask for his autograph. Kelly shook her head in disbelief. This was so surreal. How had her life led up to this moment – to sharing a car with Pelé?

At the gala, she ended up chatting to more world-class players – from Ronaldo to Messi, Gerrard and Torres.

When the FIFA Player of the Year Award was announced, Marta Vieira da Silva from Brazil won, with German player Birgit Prinz placed second, and Kelly in third place. She admired both of them greatly, especially Marta who had the flair all Brazilian world-class players seemed to possess.

'You're the best in my eyes, Kelly,' said her dad.

She smiled. 'Dad, I'm just so happy to be surrounded by these legends. Both Birgit and Marta are exceptional players. It's an honour to be just behind them. I couldn't care less where I'm placed.'

Her dad replied: 'Yeah, but it's players like you that mean women are standing up here with these legends. It's not only what you've done for football, but for women's football, Kelly. Did you think when you were kicking that ball around in the front room copying Ryan Giggs, you'd be sharing a limousine with Pelé one day or posing for FIFA pictures?'

Kelly smiled again. 'Perhaps not, but I always

knew I'd be playing football, somehow, in some way. I wanted to be the best women's player in the world. But I've come as close to that as I could – I'm behind two of the greatest female players the world has ever seen.'

But nothing could beat the day an envelope with the Queen's hallmark fell through the door at her home.

'I'm pretty sure this isn't from the taxman,' Kelly thought as she opened it.

No, it was indeed a letter from the Queen – she was to be recognised for her services to women's football. Nothing could beat this – to be thanked for her service to the country she played for. Again, these highs felt all the sweeter, when she considered the lows she'd survived over the past few years.

The big day arrived. She stood at the palace in her brand new blue dress complete with a fluffy fascinator. Well, she couldn't have gone in her football kit! As she stood two feet away from the Queen trying to take the enormity of the occasion in, she thought to herself: 'Wow, I'm Kelly, a girl from

Watford who just loved playing football... and now look at where I am.'

The Queen asked her how long she'd been playing football.

'Pretty much all my life,' replied Kelly.

It was a surreal moment as the Queen pinned the MBE to Kelly's dress, and then shook her hand. It struck her just how differently things could have been without the support of her parents and Hope Powell. As Kelly left the hall, she suddenly felt overwhelmed by it all. The memory of her as a young girl, eager to play but pushed out of boys' teams came back to her, and she burst into tears – tears of joy, pride and disbelief.

*

A message popped up on Kelly's Facebook page from Heather Mitts, her former Philadelphia Charge teammate. 'Hi Kelly! Would you be interested in coming back to play in a professional league?'

Kelly shot back: 'No, my time is done. I am not interested.'

But as rumours continued to circulate and Kelly

found out other English players were considering it, she sat down to discuss the pros and cons with her parents. She was happy at Arsenal Ladies but it was better money in the USA. And she had to admit, the team wasn't really challenging her anymore.

It was Marta Vieira da Silva and Cristiane Roziera's decision to be in the league that sealed it. These were top international players from around the world.

Her dad was uncertain, though.

'Are you sure you're making the right decision, Kelly?'

'Maybe it's time to create better memories of the US, Dad.'

Vic was disappointed to see her go but knew it would help her improve too. As did Hope, who said: 'If you play at international level, it's good for all of us ultimately. You'll be playing with, and against, the best players. That can only help the England team.'

Kelly would spend three years with the Boston Breakers team along with Arsenal's right-back Alex Scott. It felt strange to go back again. She'd been a mere kid the first time round. Now she felt so much stronger at facing anything the US threw at her this time round, with all the experiences and obstacles she'd overcome.

It felt great to be playing professionally again! At Arsenal Ladies, she was still only semi-professional – she worked at the academy during the day and was only able to train two nights a week. Here, in the US, it was her job, her life. She was a professional again with an individualised training programme. The level of playing felt faster, and more physical and technical too. She loved the outdoor lifestyle in Boston too and enjoyed kayaking and sailing on the river.

In the first league of the season, she scored eleven goals and played in all twenty-one matches.

When The Breakers played Chicago Red Stars no-one in defence could get near her. She picked up a pass from her defence and took it on down the pitch, bursting into the penalty area before hitting a perfect left-footed finish into the top corner. Defenders just couldn't keep up with her once she hit her stride, and the goalkeepers were struggling to predict which side she was going to shoot– she had gotten better at keeping them guessing and disguising her shots, right up until the last minute.

Kelly loved playing in the USA but it was Euro '09 in Finland that she was looking forward to. Hope had always said this was England's time to shine.

CHAPTER 17

WOMEN'S EUROPEAN CUP 2009

In the qualifying games for Euro 2009, England knew the Czech Republic would be tough but they managed to beat them, 5–1, after a difficult first half. Up next were Spain – they were two down by half-time but Kelly and Carney equalised.

So England were on their way to Finland.

Women's football was now taken so seriously they even had a toy mascot, Bruce, to attend all their games!

In their opening game in the championship, against Italy, the England team ran into trouble. They began well, taking the lead when Fara scored from the penalty spot, but then the game began to unravel. Kelly felt as though they weren't in sync

– they were far from playing their best. Then, with eight minutes remaining, disaster – Italy scored a wonder strike. Kelly was speechless – she knew they had to pull their game up to get through this tournament.

It got worse. When they played Russia, they were two goals down, after twenty-two minutes. Their formidable defender Casey Stoney had been suspended and Kelly could really feel her loss in this game. Russia weren't even a strong side.

'We deserve to go home if we continue playing like this,' thought Kelly as half-time loomed. She knew they had to focus on the here and now and forget the Italy game if they were to get this back.

Clearly, their self-confidence had taken a battering but as Kelly looked around and into everyone's eyes she sensed a shift. They were in a hole but it suddenly struck her that this could be the making of them. Deep down, they all knew they could do this. Kelly felt a bit of self-belief returning. More of her teammates started to get possession of the ball and she felt the pace quicken.

By half-time they were 3–2 up. What a confidence boost for England.

Kaz scored the first goal, and then assisted Eniola Aluko to make it two. They'd equalised. Some of the tension lifted but they knew they couldn't afford to get complacent – they needed some magic to shine. It was a few minutes from half-time and they needed something magical to happen. Kelly got control of the ball near the centre midfield. She looked up towards the goal, Why not try at rocketing one in, she thought? She took aim and struck the ball but the goalkeeper kicked it right back at her. Give up now or try again? It was a split-second decision. Kelly got a touch, lined up her left and lobbed it back towards the goal.

Was it too high? Would it strike the bar? Would it go over the bar? Kelly watched the ball sail, almost as if in slow motion, over the keeper's head and into the back of the net.

Oh, the relief! What a sweet time to score! The team went into half-time elated at their turnaround.

Hope wasn't smiling, though.

'You were lucky, we were 2–0 down, I thought we were going out.'

Eventually, she conceded: 'Well done girls, your fighting spirit and determination really showed through today.'

The chips had been right down, and they hadn't made it easy for themselves, but Kelly now felt they had the mental strength to overcome any glitch. A few years ago the team wouldn't have recovered from that. They now had the confidence to go forward – mentally, physically and technically. But Kelly felt weary and drained from a summer playing in America.

*

It was tough playing Finland in front of a home crowd. The England team all felt the pressure and knew their opponents could be a merciless side, particularly their striker Laura Kalmari. It was a few minutes into the game and the team wanted an early goal to get into their stride. Eni was up front ready to strike, while Kelly did what she enjoyed the most – roaming around the pitch with the ball at her feet making penetrating runs. Kelly picked up Chapman's pass from the midfield and Eni struck it home. Fara scored a second, but they weren't home and dry.

Faye White suffered a head injury and Jill Scott came on to replace her. The height of the opponents caused problems, in particular when Finland's striker Annica Sjölund put them back in the game with a goal in the first part of the second half. But England fought back though and weren't going to be intimidated. Eni got on the ball and fearlessly ran towards the defenders, leaving three or four gasping behind her as she dribbled around them. She entered the penalty box and drilled past the goalie, Tinja-Riikka Korpela, to restore the two goal lead. But they needed to hold out and fight as the Finns were putting pressure on with a series of corners. And it paid off for them, when they scored a second goal. The final twelve minutes were tense for England – but they held it together for a 3–2 win, with Rachel making a great save. They'd beaten a good team on home soil. It had been hard, but one of their best wins yet.

However, the girls were crestfallen to hear that the

BBC weren't broadcasting their quarter-final match with the Netherlands.

'I'm sorry, girls,' said Hope to the team. 'They're not going to televise it.'

'What?' the team cried.

'Come on – don't let it get you down. Let's do this!' Hope encouraged them.

Kelly knew they had a task ahead of them. The Dutch team focused on defending, so she knew they'd have to work hard to break them down. But she was given a boost when she heard their coach Vera Pauw say she thought Kelly was one of the best players in the world.

But at half-time neither side had scored. England had to be patient.

'Don't worry, girls,' said Hope at half-time, 'the breakthrough will come.'

It did come – but not until fifty-one minutes in. Kaz ran down the left flank, and passed it to Eni who cut it over to Kelly, just before a defender could reach her. Kelly caught the ball and on first touch left-booted it in to the left side of the net – GOAL!!!

It had been a long time coming but now they had a breakthrough. Kelly skidded on the turf and threw her arms up in the air shouting for joy. The team leapt around and hugged her with relief and delight. Within three minutes, striker Marlous Pieëte equalised for the Netherlands. Everyone was tired.

'Don't let it go to penalties,' thought Kelly. But she trusted that the team had a new psychological strength to pull them through. They stayed tough. Jill Scott saved the day with a header from Karen's corner kick. Pure pandemonium in the stadium! They defended to the end, didn't let their concentration go and jumped for joy as their place in the final with Germany was sealed. Wooohoooo!!!!!!!

Kelly was awarded Player of the Match, and Hope praised her. 'Yet again Kelly, you've held it together during a tough time. When you play well, you give everyone else the confidence and self-belief to pull through together.'

Kelly beamed. 'We've all learnt so much together.'

Later, while the girls relaxed and played a game of

pool, Kaz stormed through the door.

'The BBC! They're playing our match live!'

'About time!!!' Hope stuck her head round the door.

'I've got some good news', she smiled.

Their captain, Faye White, appeared behind her.
It had only been a week since she'd fractured her
cheekbone.

'They've given me the all clear guys,' said Faye.
'I can play in the final. I just need to wear this really
attractive face protective mask!'

Her teammates jumped around and threw their
mascot Bruce up in the air. They had a lot to thank
him for.

*

England were now playing in their first women's
European Championship final since 1984. That
team had lost to penalties to Germany, and twenty-
five years later, they didn't want the same thing to
happen. The team had their work cut out for them
and they knew it. They were up against some key
players, from revered world player Birgit Prinz to
midfielder Kim Kulig. A rumour started to circulate

that the Germans had already planned their celebratory victory party, which kickstarted the English girls' fighting spirit more than ever.

'We're just going to have to close them down at every opportunity,' said Hope.

'This is where we use all defending skills necessary – we can't let them attack!' said Faye. 'Don't give them any time on the ball!'

But they remembered Japan who they'd drawn against. They could do it.

Kelly walked out into the Helsinki Olympic Stadium and felt a peculiar sense of excitement and pride. She waved and said 'Hello mum' to the camera, who was watching it at home on TV.

The final started well and was fairly even but England conceded two goals within the first half-hour. But they didn't mentally fall apart as they may have done in previous matches. This was where they found their strength and didn't give up.

It was how they responded that counted. Kelly showed no fear and got up and ran into the penalty box. She cut past defenders and flicked back the ball with her left foot on the inside from the byline for Kaz to get one in.

At half-time, Hope was happy with their progress so far but the Germans kept fighting back stronger. England were 3–1 down with forty minutes to go. Something had to change. Then Kelly performed a first. She picked up the ball from Kaz and left-booted the ball into the right side of the net, past goalkeeper Nadine Angerer.

It was Kelly's first ever goal against Germany.

But after the Germans scored a fourth goal, Kelly felt some of the team's self-belief disappear. Their opponents went on to win 6–2. This time, it wasn't meant to be.

'Come on', said Kelly, to the disappointed team. 'We've got a lot to be proud of. We made it to the final!'

'Yeah,' agreed Faye, 'but if we're ever going to win we need to keep the momentum going beyond sixty minutes.'

'It's another lesson learnt,' said Kelly, 'and we're getting better all the time.'

CHAPTER 18

WOMEN'S WORLD CUP 2011

It was the Cyprus Cup and the England team were playing against Italy. Kelly loved being out there in the Mediterranean sun, and knew this was a fun chance for the team to bond in preparation for the Women's World Cup that year. But this was a particularly special day for Kelly.

Hope gathered the girls around. 'So, everyone – bit different today. Kelly will be your captain.'

'Oh yeah, why's that, then?' teased Jill. 'Think she's something special?'

'This is Kelly's one hundredth international cap. One hundredth!' I thought this would be a fitting way to celebrate it.'

'Woo hoo!' The girls whooped and cheered.

Kelly couldn't believe it. One hundred games. It all seemed such a blur as she looked back over her nearly twenty-year career.

'I suppose I'd better score a goal then, hadn't I?!' Kelly joked.

She didn't disappoint on this celebratory occasion and scored a penalty against Italy. The young and talented Ellen White, the centre-forward at Arsenal Ladies, also scored.

The team went on to beat the USA 2–1 in a friendly match before the Women's World Cup. The USA team were ranked Number 1 in the world, so Kelly knew England were now at a fantastic level, with a really good mix of experienced and new, enthusiastic players – from legend striker Rachel Yankey to goalkeeper Karen Bardsley and attacker Ellen White.

'We can compete with the best now!' she said to Hope.

'Ready for the World Cup in Germany, then?!'

'Yeah!' said Kelly.

*

'Wow!'

The girls looked out of the tour bus. Everywhere they looked, on the streets of Berlin, people were dressed in the German flag colours – red, black and gold.

'Check this out!' Kaz showed the team a special edition women's football sticker album that had been made for the World Cup.

'It's the first time they've ever done it!' said Jill Scott.

'Not sure about my hair in that picture, though!' protested Kelly.

Spirits in the England camp were high and Jill was having fun driving everyone crazy videoing behind-the-scenes footage of the team. They made up dance routines to S Club 7's 'Reach' to shake out any nervous energy. They felt confident but knew they had big games ahead of them. Kelly sensed their worry about an imminent game with Japan. Her memories of Miyama the free kick genius still seemed fresh in her mind, even though it was four years ago now. She practised visualising again to remain calm.

The England team knew that New Zealand's game

would be tough but just before the game Hope came in looking sombre. 'Rigid and predictable.' She hung up a banner with the words 'rigid and predictable' printed on it. 'This is what the New Zealand coach has said about you.'

They all shouted: 'We'll prove him wrong!'

They went out fighting with those words in mind. It was a physically tough game but they believed they could break them down as the US had. But it didn't go smoothly.

'Aaargh!' Kelly felt her ankle roll as she went to challenge Jenny Bindon the goalkeeper at a corner. She limped on throughout the game. She looked over at Kaz and Yanks. She could see they were also fed up with the number of fouls being made against them.

'I know, girls', said Hope at half-time. 'They're intentionally going for you because you're good – try and take it as a compliment!'

The girls protested: 'It's completely unfair! What sort of a game plan is that?!'

'Don't let them get to you.' Hope replied.

Jill Scott and Jess Chapman eventually both scored for England to win 2–1, but Kelly felt derailed by the pain in her ankle.

She tried to hide that it was troubling her, but they knew her too well.

'Come on Smudge, don't let it get you down,' they all rallied around her.

'How about a game of poker?' This was one of the girls' favourite tournament games.

'Nah.'

'Table tennis? Someone's gotta beat Casey!' Casey was a master with the bat.

'What about... "In it to win it"?'

This was based on an American game show that centred round teams performing ridiculous tasks.

Kelly smiled. 'Yeah, alright! Everyone get into pairs, then!'

They groaned. 'Oh no... what will it be this time?'

'Okay... have we got any spaghetti?'

'Yes!'

'How about we build a tower... using only... our teeth!'

'What???' They all fell about laughing as one by one they set about trying to achieve this.

'Go, Smithy!'

'Jill – don't record this – please!'

'Afraid I am, Smithy!'

'If you put that up on FA.com, I will not be happy.'

'They gotta know what's happening in camp!'

*

They hadn't believed their match against Japan was a sellout until they got there but the noise in the stadium eliminated any remaining doubts. Their game plan for Japan was to attack and be as aggressive as possible. It worked. Ellen and Rachel scored two terrific goals and they didn't concede any. They were overjoyed to find they'd topped the group.

Kelly joined in with the celebrations. She was so happy they'd made it to the quarter- final but she knew her troubles with her ankle were far from over. And she knew they faced France next – a tough team to beat.

As they walked out into the Bay Arena stadium to face France, they felt swamped by the sound of the French fans. Kelly turned around to them all with a smile and said: 'Remember to enjoy it! We've got to just enjoy it!' She knew it wouldn't be easy, though, and was on the lookout for striker Marie-Laure Delie – a formidable player who'd scored 23 goals in 23 appearances.

No-one scored in the first half but England could feel France piling on the pressure. Hope rallied around them at half-time: 'Be patient girls, hang on in there. You're doing great. Take your chance, you'll know the right time.'

They did. Their chance came in the fifty-eighth minute when Rachel Unitt hit a long ball forward, Kelly made contact and played it into Jill. She was twenty-five yards from the goal but without breaking stride kicked it over the head of goalkeeper Céline Deville... their first goal against France!

'The lead is ours! Yes!' The girls were ecstatic, but Kelly knew it was far from over. She felt the French increase the pressure as she tried to ignore the pain in her ankle.

'Just get through this...' she told herself. She momentarily looked in the direction of her dad, as if for comfort. It felt as though time had slowed down, even though they were playing so well defensively. Then, Hope made a decision that would be scrutinised after the match. Alex Scott and Rachel Unitt were swapped in for two younger, less experienced players.

When the French scored, Kelly felt England's team spirit break a little. How quickly fortune flipped. She couldn't play her best with this ankle and they were down to ten players due to Katie Chapman being sent off. Kelly knew if she left it would affect how they all played. Not that she wanted to leave either. She wanted to stay with her team.

'Get through, get through... we can't give up now,' she kept saying to herself. She struggled through to the inevitable penalties they'd dreaded. She was the first to put her hand up to take one, despite her ankle. She had faith she could do it, although she sensed the fear of the other players in coming forward.

Kelly's ankle was agony, but she knew she could get this done. She felt angry enough and frustrated with how the game had turned out, but she knew she could power this home. She went to take the penalty, and repeated to herself her usual mantra:

'Put the ball down in a good spot. Focus on the frame of the goal. Keep your head over the goal. And don't put it over the bar.'

'Take that!' She felt a wave of relief wash over her as she saw it slam into the back of the top right hand corner of the net. Elation! What a release! Kaz and Casey got their penalties in too, and it was 3–2 to England. Claire Rafferty missed her penalty, and then Faye stepped forward. She struck the bar.

Devastation rippled through the team. They'd not been beaten but they were going home. Their dream and hopes were dashed. Kelly realised at that moment that you can prepare as much as possible and plough your energy into doing the best that you can but ultimately, you can't plan how everything will affect you – the crowd, the stadium, the pressure, the injuries, or the sense of letting your teammates down. It seemed as if every England football team was cursed when it came to penalties.

CHAPTER 19

THE LONDON OLYMPICS

When Kelly returned from playing for the Boston
Breakers in the USA, she was really excited to re-sign
with Arsenal. She was in a film studio for ESPN TV
to promote the new Women's Super League season,
along with Steph Houghton, Alex Scott and Kim
Little. They started to work out some action shots for
the photographer.

Kelly was enjoying larking about with her
teammates. She chucked a header to Alex Scott
and started practising keepy-uppies for the camera.
However, in her excitement, she forgot about the
recent injury she'd picked up in her left foot. When
the photographer threw a ball at her she kicked it

back with her left foot on instinct. She felt immediate pain. 'Ouch!' She tried to place it on the ground but couldn't put any pressure on it all. She went to the doctor who advised immediate surgery, and she had a plate put in.

She couldn't believe she was in this position again. It was 2012, the year of the Olympics and she was desperate to play for the Great Britain team.

Her doctor asked.

'Do you want to get back to playing football as soon as possible?'

'I want it more than anything!'

Kelly had been looking forward to the Olympics since the disappointment of the last Women's World Cup. Her injury meant she had to miss out on the Women's Super League, the FA Women's Cup and Women's Champion League but she could just about cope with that – as long as she got better for the Olympics.

Kelly was scared of missing out on the chance of a lifetime but this time, she didn't allow negative thoughts to plague her as she may have done many years ago. Now, she had several coping mechanisms in place. She had learnt to quieten her mind, remain calm and accept what may or may not happen. Rather than looking bleakly into the future, she visualised herself playing for her country in London at Wembley Stadium. Her heart swelled with pride at the thought of it and immediately she felt better. She could feel positive vibes radiating throughout her entire body.

And a lot was changing in women's football. She felt it was finally being taken more seriously in the country. The first Women's Super League had been set up in 2010 and there was decent media coverage of her Arsenal games. Okay, so she might still be no way near earning what Wayne Rooney was on, but things were looking up.

The day for the call-up to the Olympics came. Had she made the squad? Kelly tried to distract herself by going to the gym. She didn't want to be waiting desperately for the call. When her phone rang she almost didn't want to answer it.

'Hello?' she said nervously.

'Kelly? It's Hope.'

'Hi Hope'. She took a deep breath and almost tried to prepare herself for the worst news.

'How'd you like to be a part of Team GB this summer?'

'Wahoo!!' Kelly leapt up and down so hard she felt a twinge in her foot again but she didn't care. She was one of six Arsenal Ladies players chosen for the squad, along with England international players Alex Scott, Ellen White, Steph Houghton and Rachel Yankey –all raring to go!

*

The Team GB kit took some getting used to. There were no three lions this time representing England, but a British shirt with the Union Jack on it. They were representing all four nations.

And this time, the eyes of the world were on them. Their match against New Zealand in Cardiff's Millennium Stadium was to be shown live on BBC One that afternoon – another indication of just how far women's football had come. And millions would be tuning in around the world. The team couldn't wait to get started.

Kelly said: 'This is our chance girls, we'd better make it a good one.'

They were excited and knew they were good enough to wow the international audience. They deserved this moment. And it felt as though the world – well, Cardiff at least – agreed. The streets were crammed with people painted in Union Jacks – everyone was cheering and clapping.

As they lined up in the stadium to sing 'God Save the Queen' Kelly could barely hold back the tears as she held her hand on her chest and tried to sing the words out as steadily as possible.

It was another moment where she looked back and reflected on just how far she'd come – a girl from Watford, who was now here playing in the Olympics, in the very year it was being hosted in her country. She didn't feel nervous now, just pure excitement.

Kelly felt the team play with a little apprehension at the beginning of the match, but a breakthrough came in the second half when Steph Houghton scored a wonderful free kick. Next day the faces of the Team GB's women's football team were splashed all over the newspapers – finally they were getting the coverage they deserved.

'Hey – check this out too!'

Casey brought in the official Team GB football programme.

'Ooh – look!' They all pointed at Kelly on the front with Tom Cleverley.

Casey teased: 'Yeah, but look who I'm with!'

Kelly laughed. 'Ryan Giggs?! That's so unfair.' The photos had actually all been shot separately but regardless, it felt good to see their images side by side with the men – attitudes towards women playing football were changing.

Their spirits were high as they watched the opening Olympics ceremony on the TV. They looked forward to their match with Cameroon, their spirits high.

It was one of their toughest matches though.

'Aaargh!' Kelly took a hit in the face from one of their opponents. 'That's going to hurt tomorrow', she thought. Rachel looked over at her and grimaced. They could all read each other's thoughts on the pitch by now – what was it with this team?

Despite the rough play, Kelly got hold of the ball and passed through to Scottish player Kim Little. Quick on her feet, she back heeled to Jill Scott who shot it in, on one touch – the three of them all danced together on the pitch.

'That referee is terrible!' they all moaned at half-time.

'We're all taking some really tough tackles, Hope!'
'Yeah, well, I know, girls. But you can cope with it.'

And it turns out they could. They conceded no goals and won 3–0. Now they faced Brazil.

CHAPTER 20

GB VERSUS BRAZIL

'London here we come!!' The team were on their way to London, they day after they qualified for the quarter-finals. As they turned into Wembley Stadium they all sang 'Reach for the Stars' by S Club 7. They'd recently filmed the entire team singing different lines from the song and it had become an internet sensation, as well as the anthem for the tournament.

'Wembley Stadium! This is it!' This is what Kelly had envisioned since her injury. They spotted famous celebrities everywhere. 'Look, it's Mo Farah!' 'Jessica Ennis!' 'OMG – Usain Bolt!'

'I don't care,' said Casey, 'as long as there's a McDonalds.'

'Yep, there is – a huge one!' said Kelly.

Jill Scott joked: 'Do you think if we asked Usain nicely, he'd run over and get us all one?! It could be a new record breaker!'

Later that evening, Kelly and Fara leaned against the pool table in the Olympic village. They faced one of their most serious matches yet – a game of doubles playing against Aaron Ramsey of Arsenal and James Tomkins from West Ham.

The boys said with a twinkle in their eye, 'Whoever loses has to make the tea'. They looked pretty laidback about their forthcoming battle.

'Oh, okay then,' said Kelly shyly, pretending to lull them into a false sense of security.

Both Kelly and Fara proceeded to clear up the table, winning the best of five games.

'No sugar in mine thanks, lads!' said Kelly.

It was good to feel this inclusive among the male players – they weren't a girl or boys' team, just both genders together enjoying and playing football for Team GB.

As they walked out into Wembley Stadium the

noise was deafening. Kelly knew the crowds would be big but she wasn't prepared for the noise or people – 70,584 in total. This wasn't about a men's match being preceded by a women's match. They were here to see women play football – their third group game of 2012. Kelly felt the pressure to do it justice. Normally, she stayed in the changing rooms to prepare herself mentally but tonight she walked around the pitch with all the girls to take in the whole experience and soak up the occasion. She saw the yellow Brazilian tops and knew that Marta, the best player in the world was out there – Kelly felt ready to beat her. They had to prove to Great Britain and the rest of the world that they were worth watching.

The team could hear 'Team GB! Team GB!' shouted over and over in the first few minutes. They all knew it was going to be a good game. But they didn't think they'd be ahead so early. Steph came up from a left-back position to find herself on the right-hand side of the six-yard box. She saw a chance as she cut past a defender and the goal opened up for her. The roar around the stadium was euphoric as it had sunk in that Team GB had scored, barely five minutes into the game. They were all in shock. Kelly had a chance to double it before half time but her shot went narrowly wide. But it didn't matter. The whistle blew to call time on the game. They'd beaten Brazil 1–0, in front of a crowd of over 70,000 and just under 4 million viewers watching on the BBC.

At the end they did the lap of honour and ran round thanking the crowd and taking in the moment. Kelly looked for her mum and dad and saw them on the halfway line, coming towards her waving and smiling, along with Glen and his girlfriend. Brazil were a tough and technical side to beat but they'd defended throughout and stuck together as a team.

This was their moment and a game they'd talk about for years to come. Kelly looked around the pitch one last time before she heard the familiar voice of her dad: 'Alright, Kell?!'

CHAPTER 21

HANGING UP HER BOOTS

Kelly jogged around St George's Park, set in hundreds of acres of Staffordshire countryside and home to England's twenty-eight national teams. Ordinarily, she loved this time alone to herself, getting in the zone before looking ahead to a day of training. But this time, as she got halfway round the pitch she felt a twinge in her knee. She'd been struggling with her ACL injury on and off for years. Normally, she'd push herself on and keep running. Instead, she came to a standstill, surveyed the beautiful sweeping hills in front of her and took out her phone.

'Kelly!' said her dad, Bernard, on the other end of the line. 'Alright love, to what do I owe this honour?'

'Hi Dad...'

She paused for a moment.

'I think I've come to a decision...'

'You've finally come to your senses and you're going to support Watford?'

Kelly laughed.

'No dad, I think it's time... my heart's not in this anymore.'

But Kelly wasn't going to hang up her boots just yet – there was still an entire season at Arsenal Ladies to look forward to.

*

It was the FA Cup Final at Wembley – Arsenal Ladies versus Chelsea Ladies. Here were two London teams with a fierce and competitive history. It was always a big deal for Arsenal to beat this team and if they won today it would be their fourteenth win.

Vic Akers looked at Kelly with a wry smile. He sensed this was one of the last times he'd see her play.

'Come on Vic,' said Kelly, 'this is a happy day for me.'

'Yeah...'

'I'm playing at Wembley, for the team I supported since I was a young kid, for the only team I've ever played for in England... my whole family are here... and there's yet another record crowd out there!'

She paused.

'There's a lot to smile about,' she carried on.

'Well, yeah, that was always your motto wasn't it? "Always play..."?'

'"...with a smile on your face..."' finished Kelly.

She continued: 'I'm going to do everything I can to help my team win today.'

The match commentators gathered in the press box to discuss the players:

'Legend is a term that's sometimes used too often but Kelly Smith is certainly that.'

'Cool, calm, clinical – her experience is so important on occasions like this.'

'She's shy and humble off pitch but a demon on it. And she can switch a game from losing to winning in a second. When she plays well it lifts everyone's spirits.'

Later that afternoon Arsenal celebrated their 1–0

victory over Chelsea. As Kelly walked up the famous Wembley steps to lift the FA Cup trophy, she knew it would be the last time she held it. She couldn't stop grinning and cheering.

*

Kelly beamed at the row of little faces all looking up at her in the classroom. She'd been asked to speak at her former primary school. When it came to question time, Kelly was overjoyed to see a wave of hands go up. She had no problem with public speaking now.

'When did you start playing football?' 'Where were you spotted?' 'Who's your biggest hero?' As she answered each question in turn, Kelly was pleased to note that just as many girls as boys were putting their hands up.

'What's the proudest moment of your entire career?' asked one girl.

Many images flashed before Kelly's eyes – meeting the Queen, scoring two goals against Japan in the World Cup, scoring a record number of goals for England... they were all achievements that she looked back on with pride. But as she looked around the faces looking up at her, she remembered what her dad had said to her all those years ago: 'You'll be a hero to young girls who want to play football some day.' She was incredibly proud that football was now the most popular female sport in the country. Finally, she answered the question.

'Well,' replied Kelly, 'coming back here to meet you lot, of course!'

Turn the page for a sneak preview of another
brilliant Ultimate Football Heroes story – KANE
by Matt and Tom Oldfield.

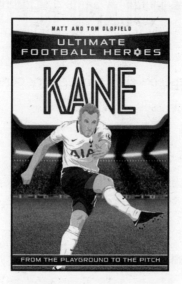

Available now!

CHAPTER ONE

ENGLAND HERO

Thursday, 5 October 2017

In the Wembley tunnel, Harry closed his eyes and soaked up the amazing atmosphere. He was back at the home of football, the stadium where he had first achieved his childhood dream of playing for England. 19 March 2015, England vs Lithuania – he remembered that game like it was yesterday. He had scored that day and now, with England facing Slovenia, he needed to do it again. As England's captain and Number 9, it was his job to shoot them to the 2018 World Cup.

'Come on, lads!' Harry called out to his teammates behind him, friends like Joe Hart, Kyle Walker and

Eric Dier. It was a real honour to be their leader.
With a victory over Slovenia, they would all be on
their way to the biggest tournament of their lives
in Russia.

Harry looked down at the young mascot by his
side and smiled at him. 'Right, let's do this!'

As the two of them led the England team out on to
the pitch, the fans clapped and cheered. Harry didn't
look up at the thousands of faces and flags; instead,
he looked down at the grass in front of him. He
was totally focused on his task: scoring goals and
beating Slovenia.

'If you get a chance, test the keeper,' Harry said
to his partners in attack, Raheem Sterling and
Marcus Rashford, before kick-off. 'I'll be there for the
rebound!'

Harry's new Premiereship season with Tottenham
Hotspur had not begun well in August, but by
September he was back to his lethal best. That
month alone, he scored an incredible 13 goals,
including two goals for England against Malta. He
could score every type of goal – tap-ins, headers, one-

on-ones, long-range shots, penalties, even free kicks. That's what made him such a dangerous striker.

With Slovenia defending well, Harry didn't get many chances in the first half. He got in good positions but the final ball never arrived.

'There's no need to panic yet,' Harry told his teammates in the dressing room. He really didn't want a repeat of England's terrible performance against Iceland at Euro 2016. That match still haunted him. 'We're good enough to win this by playing our natural game. Be patient!'

As Ryan Bertrand dribbled down the left wing, Harry sprinted towards the six-yard box. Ryan's cross didn't reach him but the ball fell to Raheem instead. His shot was going in until a defender deflected it wide.

'Unlucky!' Harry shouted, putting his hands on his head. 'Keep going, we're going to score!'

Without this kind of strong self-belief, Harry would never have made it to the top of European football. There had been lots of setbacks along the way: rejections, disappointments and bad form. But every time, Harry bounced back with crucial goals at crucial moments. That's what made him such a superstar.

A matter of seconds later, a rebound fell to him on the edge of the penalty area. Surely, this was his moment. He pulled back his left foot and curled a powerful shot towards the bottom corner. The fans were already up on their feet, ready to celebrate. Harry never missed... but this time he did. The ball flew just wide of the post. Harry couldn't believe it. He looked up at the sky and sighed.

On the sideline, England manager Gareth Southgate cheered his team on. 'That's much better – the goal is coming, lads!'

But after ninety minutes, the goal still hadn't come. The fourth official raised his board: eight minutes of injury time.

'It's not over yet, boys!' Harry shouted, to inspire his teammates.

The Slovenian goalkeeper tried to throw the ball out to his left-back but Kyle got there first. Straight away, Harry was on the move from the back post to the front post. After playing together for years at Tottenham, they knew how to score great goals.

As Kyle crossed it in, Harry used his burst of speed to get in front of the centre-back. Again, the England supporters stood and waited anxiously. The ball was perfect and Harry stretched out his long right leg to meet it. The keeper got a touch on his shot but he couldn't keep it out.

GOAL!

He had done it! Joy, relief, pride – Harry felt every emotion as he ran towards the fans. This time, he hadn't let them down. He held up the Three Lions on his shirt and screamed until his throat got sore.

'Captain to the rescue!' Kyle laughed as they hugged by the corner flag.

'No, it was all thanks to you!' Harry replied.

At the final whistle, he threw his arms up in the air. It was a phenomenal feeling to qualify for the 2018 World Cup. He couldn't wait to lead England to glory.

'We are off to Russia!' a voice shouted over the loudspeakers and the whole stadium cheered.

- 🏆 Fifth in 2006 FIFA Women's World Player of the Year: 2006
- 🏆 Fourth in 2007 FIFA Women's World Player of the Year: 2007
- 🏆 Fifth in 2008 FIFA Women's World Player of the Year: 2008
- 🏆 Third in the 2009 FIFA Women's World Player of the Year: 2009
- 🏆 PFA Special Achievement Award: 2017

SMITH

10 & 14

THE FACTS

NAME: Kelly Smith
DATE OF BIRTH: 29 Oct 1978
AGE: 39
PLACE OF BIRTH: Watford, London
NATIONALITY: England
POSITION: ST
BEST FRIENDS: Her dad, Bernard
MAIN CLUB: Arsenal

THE STATS

Height (cm):	**168**
Club appearances:	**162**
Club goals:	**116**
International appearances:	**113**
International goals:	**46**
International trophies:	**0**
Womens's World Player of the Year:	
	3rd place – 2009, 4th – 2007, 5th – 2006, 2008

★ ★ ★ **HERO RATING: 90** ★ ★ ★

GREATEST MOMENTS

Type and search the web links to see the magic for yourself!

28 AUGUST 2009
ENGLAND 3-2 RUSSIA

https://www.youtube.com/watch?v=nTvemTond98
After a dismal start to the game for England in this 2009 European Championship match, Russia get ahead with a 2-0 lead. But the England team fight back to equalise. With just a few minutes to go before the whistle blows for half time, Kelly scores an incredible long-range goal to put England in the lead and on the way to a silver medal.

2 — 16 SEPTEMBER 2010
ENGLAND 3-2 SWITZERLAND

https://www.youtube.com/watch?v=Ljs50YP2MvA
Kelly's left boot shines yet again to ensure a
comfortable win against Switzerland that ensures
England qualifies for the World Cup in 2011. But
perhaps more importantly, it's this match that makes
her England's all-time record goal scorer – with her
41st international goal.

3 — 11 SEPTEMBER 2007
ENGLAND 2-2 JAPAN

https://www.youtube.com/watch?v=5M6j29Zr7-I
Kelly's reputation for turning a losing game around
was cemented in this crucial match against Japan.
With England 1–0 down, she scores two incredible
goals towards the end of the second half – with first
her left and then right foot. Japan go on to equalise
but Kelly's goals keep England in the World Cup
through to the quarter-finals.

1 JUNE 2014
ARSENAL 2-0 EVERTON

4

https://www.youtube.com/watch?v=lbckj_h2cf0

Kelly's famous left boot steals the show yet again with an incredible free kick that puts Arsenal in the lead in the FA Cup Final. She then goes on to set up the second goal for Japanese midfielder Yukari Kinga.

PLAY LIKE YOUR HEROES

SEE IT HERE **You Tube**

https://www.youtube.com/watch?v=be_oRTAOltY

STEP 1: Run into the box, angling to the right and making sure you're in front of the defender, as the ball comes into you.

STEP 2: Turn to face the incoming pass and, as the ball rolls towards you, redirect it with a touch from the inside of your left foot. It should roll behind your right foot, changing direction and totally baffling the defender!

STEP 3: Bounce off your left leg, and sprint off after the ball. The defender will now be a tangle of limbs on the floor.

STEP 4: Your strength will hold off any remaining challenges, before you slot coolly past the keeper. No chance!

STEP 5: Take off your boot and kiss it as you run to the corner flat to celebrate. Hero!

TEST YOUR KNOWLEDGE

QUESTIONS

1. What football game did Kelly play with the lads at her school?

2. What was the name of the football club that Kelly first played for?

3. What was Kelly's favourite meal?

4. Who took Kelly to her first match at Highbury?

5. Which Manchester United player did Kelly model her style of playing on?

6. Who managed Pinner Park and wanted to encourage more girls to play football?

7. Who did Kelly play against in her senior debut with Wembley Ladies?

8. Which US football team did Kelly sign a three-year scholarship with?

9. Which French striker did Kelly form a close friend ship with?

10. What number shirt did Kelly want to wear when she returned to Arsenal Ladies?

11. Who nearly scored in the first half-hour against Japan in the 2007 Women's World Cup?

12. Which TV chat show did Kelly appear on after the Women's World Cup?

13. Kelly injured her ankle in which World Cup 2011 game?

14. In which stadium did Team GB play New Zealand in the London 2012 Olympics?

Answers below. . . No cheating!

1. *King of the Square* 2. *Garston Boys* 3. *Shepherd's pie* 4. *Russ Cawson* 5. *Ryan Giggs* 6. *Norman Burns* 7. *The Doncaster Belles* 8. *Seton Hall Pirates* 9. *Marinette Pichon* 10. *Number 8* 11. *Eniola Aluko* 12. *The Jonathan Ross Show* 13. *New Zealand* 14. *Cardiff's Millennium Stadium*

HAVE YOU GOT THEM ALL?

This summer, the world's best footballers will pull on their country's colours to go head to head for the ultimate prize – the FIFA Women's World Cup.

Celebrate by making sure you read the stories of three more Ultimate Football Heroes!